STREET
GAMES

STREET
GAMES
Alan Milberg

McGraw-Hill Book Company
New York   St. Louis   San Francisco   Dusseldorf
London   Mexico   Sydney   Toronto

1 2 3 4 5 6 7 8 9 H A H A 7 9 8 7 6

Library of Congress Cataloging in Publication Data
Milberg, Alan.
  Street games.
  SUMMARY: Explores the origins, rules, variations, lingo, records, and playing fields of red rover, jacks, leapfrog, and many other street games.
  1. Games. [1. Games] I. Title.
GV1203.M63   790   74-22605
ISBN 0-07-041915-9
ISBN 0-07-041916-7 pbk.

Acknowledgements

Preface: "Dodo and the Long Tale" from *Alice's Adventures in Wonderland,* Lewis Carroll, copyright © 1963 by the Macmillan Company. Permission of Macmillan Publishing Company, Inc. **Page 20:** "Choosing Sides," P.V.E. Ivory, *Century Magazine,* July, 1915. **Page 21:** "A Matching Game," Jan-Ken-Pon, Japan, 1950. **Page 28:** "Horseshoes," *News from Home,* September, 1952, the Home Insurance Company. **Page 31:** "Playing at Ball" from *Egypt,* George Moritz Ebers, copyright 1885, Cassell & Co. Ltd., London. **Page 32:** "Exercises of the Youths" from *The New World,* Stefan Lorant, copyright 1946, Duell, New York. **Page 35:** Mosaic in the Villa Casale (Piazza Armerina) from *Sicily,* Pierre Sebilleau, copyright © 1968, Editions B. Arthaud Sarl. **Page 36:** "Hoodman's Blind" from a fourteenth-century manuscript. Bodleian Library, Oxford. **Page 37:** "Blindman's Bluff," "Francisco Goya, El Prado Museum, Madrid. **Page 40:** "Playing at Hockey," bas-relief conserved at National Archaeological Museum, Athens. **Page 43:** "Cat's Cradle" by Gabriel Bely from *Fun with Your Fingers,* Harry Helfman, copyright © 1968 by William Morrow & Co., Inc. **Page 45:** Adapted from "The Leashing of Lochiel's Dogs," New York Public Library Picture Collection. **Page 64:** "Pirate" from *L'Illustration,* December 1, 1928. Permission Baschet & Cie., Paris. **Page 64–66:** Rules for Mumbly-peg from *88 Successful Play Activities,* copyright by the National Recreation and Park Association. **Page 65:** "Development of Jackknife" from U.S. National Museum No. 2404, Vol. 60, 1922, Government Printing Office. **Page 67:** Knucklebones and Dice, the British Museum, London. **Page 67:** Two Knucklebones Players, the British Museum, London. **Page 68–71:** Courtesy the National Recreation and Park Association.

Page 78: "Humpty Dumpty's analysis of Jabberwocky" from *Through the Looking Glass,* Lewis Carroll, 1941 edition by Heritage Press. **Page 79:** "Dactylology" from *Third New International Dictionary,* copyright © 1971. Used by permission of G. & C. Merriam Co., Publishers of the Merriam-Webster Dictionaries. **Page 85:** Restoration of a Neanderthal Man, Field Museum of Natural History, Chicago. **Page 85:** From *Splendor Solis,* the British Museum, London. **Page 86:** "Jeux de Crecerelle, Moulinet, et Autres" from *Histoire des Jouets,* Henry René d'Allemagne, copyright 1902 by Librairie Hachette, Paris. **Page 86:** "Kinder-Spiel/ober Spiegel diefer Beiten," New York Public Library Picture Collection. **Page 87:** "Les Récréations Comiques dans la rue Saint-Antoine," Henry René d'Allemagne, copyright 1928, Schemit, Paris. **Page 91:** "Dressing Up," *Hearth and Home,* October 11, 1873. **Page 92:** *The Little Pretty Pocketbook,* the British Museum, London. **Page 92:** "Marbles in Egypt," Broughton, *Outing,* May, 1901. **Page 93:** Rules for Marbles, Veterans of Foreign Wars National Marble Program Booklet by permission of the Veterans of Foreign Wars of the United States. **Page 95:** Ten different marbles, courtesy Hammermill Paper Company. **Page 95:** "The cheat at marbles" from *Les Jeux D-Enfants,* copyright 1850, the Bodleian Library, Oxford. **Page 97:** Thirteenth-century wood engraving, the Bodleian Library, Oxford. **Page 99:** London Bridge before 1561, New York Public Library Picture Collection. **Page 99:** Tower Bridge, London Stereoscopic & Photographic Co., Ltd. **Page 101:** "Leapfrog," engraving by Francis Hayman, 1854, the British Museum, London. **Page 107:** "Boys Skipping," circa 1850, the Court Bookshop, London. **Page 107:** "French Children Skipping Rope," the Bodleian Library, Oxford.

Page 110: "Football Played at the Market Place," the Beck Engraving Company, Incorporated, New York, Philadelphia and Atlanta. **Page 111:** Yale Football Team, 1894, *Yale Pot Pourri, 1894,* Yale University, New Haven. **Page 116:** "Ludus Quem Itali Appellant il Calcio," engraving by Bertelli, reprinted 1903, Librairie Hachette, Paris. **Page 117:** "Hopscotch," eighteenth-century engraving, Messrs. W. T. Spencer collection. **Page 119:** "Children at Play," illustration by Jan Balet, *Graphis,* No. 51, 1954, Amstutz & Herdag, Zurich. **Page 118–122:** Rules for Hopscotch from *88 Successful Play Activities,* copyright by the National Recreation and Park Association. **Page 123:** Rules for French Hopscotch, adapted from St. Hubert's, the Riviera School, Cannes. **Page 131:** Knives used by the Franks, gift of J. Pierpont Morgan, 1917, the Metropolitan Museum of Art, New York. **Page 140–141:** "Kinderspiele," Pieter Brueghel, Kunsthistorisches Museum, Vienna. **Page 149–151:** Rules for Wiffle® Ball, courtesy The Wiffle® Ball Inc. Wiffle® is a registered trademark owned by The Wiffle Ball, Inc. **Page 153:** "Chestnutting," Winslow Homer, *Every Saturday,* October 29, 1870. **Page 159:** *Rosencrantz and Guildenstern,* Tom Stoppard, copyright © 1967 by Tom Stoppard. Reprinted by permission of Grove Press, Inc. **Page 159–161:** Coins, U.S. Mint. **Page 168:** "Roman d'Alexandre, fourteenth century," The Bodleian Library, Oxford. **Page 169:** "Buck-buck, how many fingers have I got up?" The Bodleian Library, Oxford.

Page 176: "Who Will Bell the Cat?" *Punch,* 1853. **Page 185:** "New York City Life, 1931," New York Public Library Picture Collection. **Page 187:** Photo by Hans Hildenbrand, 1933. **Page 194:** Safety Patrol Badge, American Automobile Association. **Page 196:** School Safety Patrol members receiving Distinguished Service medals, *New York Motorist,* Automobile Club of New York. **Page 197:** "Dutch Children at Play" from *Hovwelick: A Book of Emblems,* Jacob Cats, circa 1642. **Page 202:** "A Red Cross Nurse," Maud Humphrey, 1898, U.S. Library of Congress. **Page 203:** Hula-hoop® Champion Cydni Feaster, Vanguard Photography, courtesy WHAM-O Manufacturing Company. **Page 210:** Baseball card, Topps Chewing Gum, Inc., copyright William Boyd, 1950. **Page 211, 214–217:** Baseball cards, Topps Chewing Gum Inc. **Page 212–213:** Dixie Cup covers, American Can Company. **Page 222:** Holyoke Basketball Team, Holyoke Yearbook, *The Camarada,* 1911. **Page 224:** Relief der Cozumalhuapa-Kultur (Guatemala) , Museum für Völkerkunde, Berlin, **Page 238:** *Manners and Customs,* I, Wilkinson, Plon Nourritt, Paris. **Page 259:** "Discobulus," Myron, Museo Delle Terme, Rome. **Page 260–262:** IFA Proficiency Manual for Frisbee®, International Frisbee® Association and WHAM-O Manufacturing Company. **Page 263–267:** Ultimate Frisbee® Rules, copyright Columbia High School, Maplewood, New Jersey. **Page 265:** Ryan and Tatum O'Neal, Vanguard Photography, courtesy WHAM-O Manufacturing Company. **Page 272 (bottom):** *New York Daily News.* **Page 273 (top):** *Los Angeles Times.* **Page 273 (middle, "Spaldeen Olympiad"):** *The New York Times.* **Pages 272–273 (bottom):** Courtesy Korvettes. **Page 281:** UNICEF cards, contributed by Lewitt-Him of London, courtesy United Nations International Children's Emergency Fund.

In addition, I am most grateful to the following people and organizations for the research aid and materials they provided: Gladding-Vitro Aagate, Parkersburg, West Virginia (Marbles); Edward Stern and the Crown, Cork and Seal Co., Inc. (Skelly); Robert Hughes and the Wheeling Corrugating Co. (Basketball); Stephen Schwartz and Liss Public Relations, Inc. (Flipping Cards); Donald Prescott and the National Soft Drink Association (Skelly); R. W. Michaels and the Clow Corp., Oskaloosa, Iowa (Hydrants); North Pacific Products Inc., Bend, Oregon (Fads); Park Plastics Co. (Fads); Clare Atwood of Field Enterprises (Marbles); Borden Corp. (Filberts); U.S. Dept. of Transportation, Federal Highway Authority (Highway Statistics); Baseball Hall of Fame, Cooperstown, New York (World Records); Jay Mannis (Flipping Cards); Anthony Furman, Inc. (Street Olympics); Marjorie Reed (Fashions); Lois Leveman (Photo Research); J. Daphne Pinkos (Research).

I would like to thank the following for their help on the section on Law and providing information about street games in their part of the country: Harry Connick, D.A. Parish of Orleans (State of Louisiana); Dale Tooley, D.A. (Denver, Colorado); Isador Kranzal, Asst. D.A.

(Philadelphia, Pennsylvania); Ronald Walker, Asst. City Attorney (Albuquerque, New Mexico); Robert W. Allen, Asst. City Attorney (Cheyenne, Wyoming); Christopher T. Bayley, Prosecuting Attorney, and Larry Johnson (King County, Seattle, Washington); Carl J. Nemelka, City Attorney, and Ronald Bollinger, Dep. County Attorney (Salt Lake City, Utah); Arthur N. Bishop, Asst. Prosecuting Attorney, and Patricia J. Boyle, Principal Attorney, Research, Training and Appeals, County of Wayne (Detroit, Michigan); Douglas A. McIninch, Asst. County Attorney (Hillsborough County, New Hampshire); Dino J. Fulgoni, Head, Planning and Training Division (County of Los Angeles, California); Can Murdock, Asst. D.A. (Oklahoma City, Oklahoma); Jonathan L. Goldstein, U.S. Attorney, and Laurence R. Maddock, Asst. U.S. Attorney (Newark, New Jersey); Carol Vance, D.A. (Harris County, Texas); Max P. Zall, City Attorney and Thomas A. Gilliam, Asst. City Attorney (City and County of Denver, Colorado); Beth T. Ahlstrom, Jr., Asst. County and Prosecuting Attorney (Laramie County, Wyoming); John O. Garaas, State Attorney (Cass County, North Dakota); Dominich R. Carnovale, Chief Criminal Division (County of Wayne, Detroit, Michigan).

The following schools rendered material which was extremely useful, above and beyond my statewide survey: Thanks to Nancy Rotwein and the Francisco Junior High School, Baltimore, Maryland: Gail Manin and the Nursery School, Amherst, Mass.; and the Washington School, Berkeley, California.

I got background material from the works of the following authors in this field: Henry Bett, Paul Brewster, Stewart Culin, Alice Bertha Gomme, Peter and Iona Opie, Joseph Strutt, Brian Sutton-Smith, and W. W. Newell.

The photographs on pages 191 and 223 were taken by Ira Berger. George Webber and Ira Berger were most helpful with the photographic processing, and I thank them both.

Above all, I'd like to thank my editor, Alice Acheson. What can one say in a sentence or two? At the very least she's as sharp as her pencils.

One final note: The letters from well-known people whose names are printed in italics are taken from telephone interviews, letters, or information given in their behalf. I thank all of these people who sent letters or photographs.

Special Thanks to:

Greg, Rachel, Rifka, Elizabeth, Amanda, Francesca, Piet, Katy, Andy, David, Susan, Susie, Suzanne, Sue, Suzy, Sussana, Paula, Mindy, Kevin, Leslie, Lesli, Yancy, Marjorie, Niomi, Eli, Nina, Che, Jerry, Sandy, Ron, Rebecca, Marcel, Ronald, Mary Robyn, Neal, Nancy, Mara, Jenny, Abby, Janet, Dan, Debbie, Deborah, Debby, Deb, Cathy, Billy, Johnny, Jamie, Jill, Rachel, Kieth, Dee, Jim, Laura, Ashley, Tommy, Morris, Irv, John, Lester, Philip, Jose, Boo, Tina, Israel, Pearl, Kent, Larry, Joanne, Gail, Stephen, Steven, Betty, Betsy, Norman, Juan, Dominic, Angela, Jack, Andrew, Meredith, Stan, Georgio, Yank, Lucia, Joel, Mel, Wally, Pat, Donald, Jerold, Ellen, Joshua, Richard, Ray, George, Pam, Joey, Giovanni, Marlene, Frankie, Amy, Rema, Mike, Kenny, Iris, Preston, Fred, Denny, Sharon, Karen, Ralph, Paul, Lee, Adam, Rita, Martha, Robert, Bobby, Gary, Joyce, Mickey, Barry, Alice, Allison, Morris, Ginny, Patrica, Marsha, Gloria, Murray, Jody, Marilyn, Gene, Fernando, Pauline, Edward, Barbara, Dana, Ian, Laurel, June, Colin, Danny, Peter, Anne, Jessie, Ricky, Jeff, Laurence, Victor, Bonnie, Andre, George, Virginia, Pancho, Rod, Julie, Sally, Barkley, Marcia, Rhona, Herb, Judy, Hank, Hal, Howard, Benett, Leo, Joan, Faye, Arthur, Julia, Lois, Fitz, Vinnie, Sammy, Ruth, Allen, Michael, Amy, Reema, Dick, Jane, Roy, Alberto, Linda, Annette, Doris, Albert, Rocky, Johnathan, Jodi, Chuck, Raymond, Jimmy, Pedro, Harry, Helene, Warren, Blanche, Aaron, Liz, Lisa, Caren, Clark, Charlie, Art, Ella, Sidney, Georgette, Rhoda, Muffin, Harlee, Mark, Bessie, Marcia, Eton, Magrite, Robin, Carol, Carolyn, Gerry, Russell, Stephanie, Lou, Jan, Lorraine, Lorna, Roberta, Karl, Yee, Gilbert, Leda, Mimsey, Pizza, Doug, Sadie, Mildred, Gregg, Max, Moshe, Beth, Carl, Eve, Alma, Sy, Shirley, Cindy, Robert, Lee, Marc and Suzzane, Jackie, Joel, Cynda, Claire, Michelle, Josie, Phyllis, Poopers, Helen, Flodrick, Harvey, Bella, Alec, Henry, Dee, Daisy.

Very Special Thanks to:
Mother, Father, Emily, Cousin Lynn, Barry and the West Side Camera Boys, Kim, Florence, Edith Duvall, Larry Gadd and Ginger Barber.

Dedication

To my
Brother and Sisters
Danny, Anne and Sandy
for the times we played together -
They were too few.

TABLE OF CONTENTS—THE GAME

Preface

Freddy, Linda, "Stretch," and I, old childhood friends, met for dinner two years ago. Sipping coffee, we talked about our teachers and how we never imagined them in casual clothes, having first names, or ever being kids. The waiter approached the table and held the check in the air, trying to feel out who would pick up the tab. Freddy suddenly said, "Not it!,"and we each followed with "Not it! Not it! Not it!" in rapid succession, as if we really thought we could get out of paying the check by not being the last echo. It worked well years ago. We laughed quietly and split the check four ways.

While Freddy did the math, Linda asked me whether or not kids still played her favorite game, Giant Steps. With a degree of confidence, I assured her, "Probably not." *Our* games were reserved for the neighborhood and unknown to kids in other cities, states, or countries. In fact, not only was I sure kids didn't play Giant Steps, Saluggi, and Spud—if indeed there were two or three kids out there in "street land" playing our childhood games—I was positive they weren't doing it according to the rules we had known in older and better times. Admittedly. I was never quite sure how we knew all the rules, but they seemed self-evident.

> *"What is a caucus-race?" said Alice . . .*
> *"Why" said the Dodo, "the best way to explain it is to do it." . . .*
> *First it marked a race course, in a sort of circle, ("the exact shape doesn't matter," it said) then all the party were placed along the course, here and there. There was no "One, two, three, and away!" but they began running when they liked, and left off when they liked, so it was not easy to know when the race was over. However, when they had been running half an hour or so, and were quite dry again, the Dodo suddenly called out, "The race is over!" and they all crowded round it, panting, and asking, "But who has won?"*
> *Dodo and the Long Tale*
> Alice's Adventures in Wonderland
> *by Lewis Carroll*

Like the Dodo, we knew how to play these games—and when "the race is over"—and were quite sure our parents or grandparents didn't; they wouldn't understand what we were doing or how we derived pleasure from such pastimes. We cared little for tradition. Our street games had no long history, more precisely, no history at all. I was wrong.

Remembering the dinner conversation, one incident at the restaurant bothered me. The waiter laughed with us as if he understood the nostalgic kick from our "Not it!" dominos. Did he? Were there others besides Freddy, Linda, "Stretch," and now, the waiter?

As I drove home, for the first time I noticed that kids were playing in the streets, playing *our* games! We were not unique. There were others.

I did not want to pry further into the matter. I wanted to hold onto the skipping rhymes, block rituals, and secret codes which I thought were only ours. But I did probe, just to find out what made our past seem so novel.

Looking back, I was not, as they say, a natural athlete. Yet with some internal determination, gentle parental prodding, and lack of many viable alternatives, I made the big step out onto the playing field. It had no bases, foul lines, yard markers, nets, or baskets. It had grass, pavement, (lots of) dirt, lampposts, trees, and curbs which in a magic turn were transformed into bounderies, goals, bridges, and safety zones.

I, like many other kids, found comfort in competing without bleachers filled with cheering parents. I did not have to perform or act out their ambitions—only my own. Though completely taken with Giant Steps, Red Light–Green Light, Statues, and Curb Ball, I kept this excitement well concealed from parents. Perhaps they caught on when I responded to dinner call after seven or eight hours in the "field" with, "Aw, just five more minutes." Granted these were not the most athletic adventures, but I began to feel like a sporting fellow—and what a neat time I was having at that!

It was this "fun," the electric moments, that drew me to street games years ago. The magnetism lay in what I and my friends put of ourselves into the games. The rules were only attempts to keep us civilized while we played, as all children do, with uncivilized vigor, rigor, and enthusiasm.

Through playing, a well-defined value system evolved. Those who were disliked were sentenced to being "it" in every game and New Kids were lucky to survive at all. The better athletes or popular kids were the captains. Everyone, whatever their capability, had a place in the playing field—the "Peter Principle" of childhood. What we learn, after all, we learn early, and it all comes out in the games we play.

Wondering where these games came from, it surprised me that indeed our grandparents—and their grandparents—had played them here and in the Old World. Upon reaching America, through time and over space, the games often differed radically from the originals. Names, symbolisms, and meaning often changed, adapted by each succeeding generation. Nevertheless, there were and are striking similarities.

By now, all aspects of street games fascinated me. No longer crushed because my childhood pastimes were not unique, but universal, it was time to look elsewhere through interviews, questionnaires, and my camera.

Who played what, when, where? Hundreds of people from four to ninety-nine were surveyed; some traveled back in their memories, forty, fifty—even more—years or simply the day before the interview. Selling lemonade, Hide and Seek, Ghost, and Doctor, with peanut butter sandwiches as the grand finale, became fresh recollections. The most vivid memories were the competitive games or the improvisational ones with the rhythmic jazz upbeat of the street.

After all these interviews, it was time for my camera to capture remembered moments. Giant Steps, Saluggi, and Spud were all out there, but a new generation, unconsciously creating their own memories, were taking our place.

Though local rules, names, and rituals varied across the country, I found kids today, as they did thousands of years ago, are still hiding, seeking, racing, peeking; dodging, tagging, catching, snagging; blinking, staring, sometimes caring—Time out!—choosing, fleeing, losing, being; slapping, clapping, throwing, growing; eeny, meany, miny, mo-ing; tugging, slugging, even hugging.

I had a notebook filled with interviews and several hundred photographs on my desk. Wanting to put them together in a book, but needing documentation, I sent questionnaires to 350 schools, nursery through college; wrote inquiries to doctors, toy manufacturers, and recreational organizations; researched historical documents; viewed paintings, sculptures, old engravings, and archeological artifacts; and contacted district attorneys in every major city across the nation. This information, when added to the games already organized into four historical periods, satisfied my new conception of street games, and a few general patterns emerged.

In rural areas, open playing fields of grass or hard dirt present less restriction—of space. Here, however, the games tend to be more structured and community groups promote organized team sports. Accordingly, rural kids adapt their play.

Urban young, by contrast, find themselves generally limited to set-off areas—or busy streets—that offer their own lines of constraint. Confinement becomes a part of the play. Organization is coincidental, and community participation (if any) is restricted to one block or small clique. But rural or urban, fun is the name of the game. Indeed, "game" is a derivative of the Old English *gamen*, meaning fun.

City or country, the true villain of the street game today is the car. In the country, by mandate of concerned parents, all games must be played on grassy yards or quiet streets. In the city, parents resign themselves to the realization that such dangers are a fact of city life and try to live with it.

In the past it was difficult for a girl to play a "boys'" game without being cast as a "tomboy", or for a boy to play a "girls'" game without facing ridicule and the nickname "sissy". Though in some places "boys'" and "girls'" games still exist, these roles are rapidly dissolving and this book treats them just as games.

The calendar for outdoor play is, of course, largely dictated by climate; but daylight-saving time seems to be opening day for most, with outdoor running and shouting waning with the coming of the school bus in September. By Thanksgiving, caught in by frosted windowpanes, play life turns inward to the home, family, and school.

Then it's the long wait for spring, almost as long as the year between the fifth and sixth birthday, before the windows open again and one can hear the slap of the jump rope and the bounce of the spaldeen.

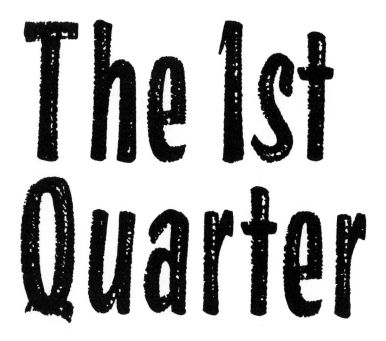

The 1st Quarter

CHOOSING SIDES

LANGUAGE

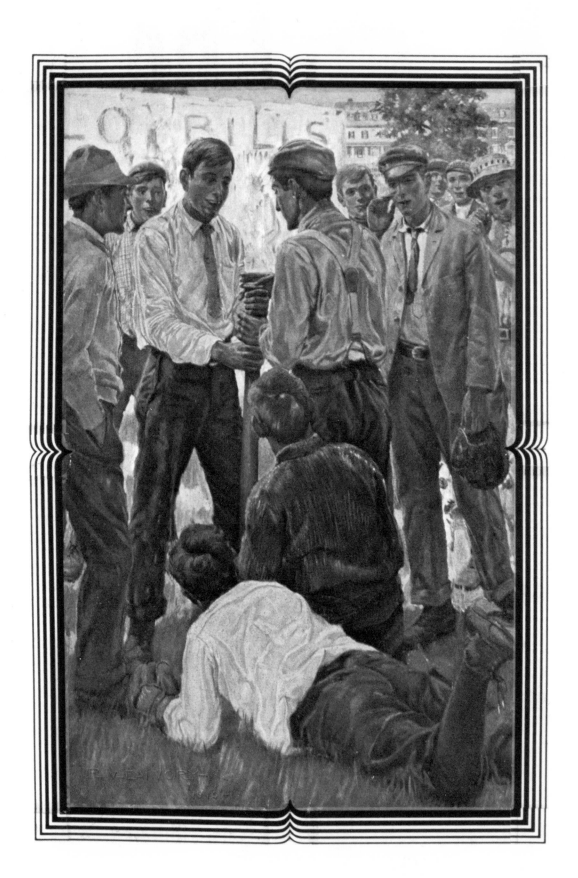

CHOOSING SIDES

Not It

This is the all-time, all-star winner for choosing one loner, chaser, caller, or someone for any other undesirable role in a game. For those who have difficulty making friends, this method can reinforce lack of confidence in the course of a game of Tag.

Casually, one kind friend asks, "Do you wanna play Tag or Spud?" Then this seemingly innocent question, like Sonar, reaches the ears of all those within shouting distance. The feedback, a fierce competition of voices shrieking, "Not it! -- Not it! -- Not it!" bouncing back and forth, until the last echo of "Not it!" is in fact "IT."

"Not it" isn't exactly the democratic process, but it expedites matters quickly.

Schimelecha, Draw a Circle

This process precedes games such as Blindman's Bluff, Hide and Seek, Tag, etc. Whoever is chosen "it," hides his eyes and faces a wall or lamppost. Then one other player draws a circle on "it's" back, while chanting:

> *Draw a shimelecha (el) or circle*
> *On the old man's back*
> *And put a finger in it (or "Someone sticks his finger in it.")*

On the last line of the chant, another member (sometimes the person who is drawing) sticks--actually thrusts would be more accurate--his finger into the back. "It" turns around and tries to guess who's finger did it. The group helps him out by chanting in nasal unison, "My finger did it; my finger did it."

If "it" guesses correctly who stuck his finger in, then the culprit becomes "it." This process, at least, gives the elected "it" a second chance, however remote, to decline the honor.

The "second-chance method," by guessing who hit the victim in the back, has been in practice over 4,000 years. It was depicted in wall paintings of Ancient Egyptian tombs dating from over 2,000 years before the birth of Christ. There are biblical references to the game in the New Testament. During the age of Golden Greece and the Middle Ages, the pastime was a game in itself, with specific tasks for the players to do once the guessing was over. Today it is known variously as: Draw a Snake Upon Your Back, Tap the Ice Box, Draw a Circle, and Stroke the Bambino.

DECISION MAKING BETWEEN *TWO*

In an effort to administer fairness, decide who's captain, who gets the sunny side, who's up first, etc., between two or more players, several colorful methods have been instituted -- but all are a bit short of *juris prudence.*

Heads or Tails

One of two players calls out heads or tails after the coin has been flipped into the air. On whichever side the coin lands decides the matter.

Odds or Evens

Again, this is between two players and the outcome is left in the hands of fate. One player calls "odds" or "evens" and the shooting begins. The two adversaries face each other and swing their fists, counting, "Once, twice, three -- shoot!" It sounds more violent than it is. On the third count, there is a downward motion of the forearm, and on the word "shoot," each player releases one or two fingers from his clenched fist. Each player must decide how many fingers he will show. Whoever called the right combination of fingers shown wins the match. A player has to win two out of three matches to win his "freedom of choice."

Whoever wins immediately ends the play-off with a guarantee clause, such as "No taxes, no nothing!" to insure his win is fair and square, with no "if's, and's, or but's."

Generally, it is better for a player to call "evens" -- his odds are two-to-one.

The Odd Finger

This ideally is designed for three players, though four can participate. More than four, and the players might as well draw swords.

The threesome form a circle and recite the "odds and evens" chant, adding the phrase, "and the odd finger is out." On the word "out," all the players show one or two fingers. Should all three throw two's or one's, the procedure is repeated until one hand's show of fingers defects from the status quo. The remaining two shooters fight it out by doing "odds and evens."

Rock, Scissors, Paper

This is "Odds and Evens" with a twist. Each player has a choice of throwing one of three symbols -- all of which have an advantage.

    Rock (clenched fist) -- *rock dulls scissors*

    Scissors (two fingers spread apart) -- *scissors cut paper*

    Paper (open palm) -- *paper covers rock*

Summary: Rock wins over scissors, but loses to paper; scissors wins over paper, but loses to rock.

The chant is "Rock, paper, scissors!" and the show of hands flourishes on the word "scissors." In some parts of the country, in keeping with certain social customs, punitive action is taken against the loser, adding more zing to the game. The loser rolls up his sleeves, unless he is wearing a T-shirt, and awaits his consequence. The winner licks his two forefingers and applies them forcefully to his opponent's forearm or wrist. (The stinging slap is a zapper.)

Which Hand

This is a game of luck, very much along the line of The Lady or the Tiger. One person holds his hands behind his back with a pebble or some other small object enclosed in either the left or right hand. Then any player has a 50-50 chance at guessing which hand has the M&M peanuts or pebble. It's uncomplicated and requires no skill.

Beware though -- there are those who even cheat behind their own backs.

The Bat

In ball games, where a stick or bat is readily available, two agile players walk to the center of the street, recreating the mood of "Bad Day at Black Rock." The tension builds as the stick holder, with stick in hand, prepares to throw up (the stick of course). The other player catches the airborne stick with one hand.

Then each player, in turn, moves hand-over-hand up the stick until the summit is reached. The top hand wins and gets first "pick." However, if there is enough room at the top of the bat or stick for a player to grasp it in his fingers, the match continues. First, the gripping player with bat in hand, must swing it around his head, assuring his total control of the stick. However, if there is still doubt, the stick holder must give his opponent the opportunity to kick the stick out of his hand. If the stick stays in his clutches, the battle is over, and the opponent walks, conceding, quietly away.

Drawing Straws or Sticks

One person gathers as many sticks or straws as there are players. One of the sticks must be shorter than all the others. The player who gathered them usually holds them in his hand, disguising their lengths. Whoever picks the shortest stick is eliminated from the group or is picked for a terrible job in the game. In either case, the loser gets the short end of the stick.

One Potato, Two Potato

This method of elimination purports to be the ultimate in fairness. In reality, it only takes longer, seems fair, and gives everyone less time to play the game.

Everyone forms a circle, and each person has an equal chance of staying in the winning circle. One person is designated the caller through general consent or by some other method of choosing. (A day could easily go by with series of "choosing procedures" alone.) The caller recites the Potato Chant:

> *One potato, two potato,*
> *Three potato, four;*
> *Five potato, six potato,*
> *Seven potato, more!*

At the same time, the caller is tapping the hands of the players, one hand on each number. The hand tapped on the word "more" is dropped from the circle. After a person has had both hands tapped (in some cases, feet too), he is eliminated from the game. Should the caller tap himself out, the person on his right takes over as poet laureate.

There is always one person with a good head for permutation who catches on to the sequence and figures out the end result as soon as the chanting begins. To outwit such clever individuals, a set of variations have been devised to constantly change the potato pattern and increase suspense.

> *My dog died last night.*
> *What color was his blood?*

Every word is a tap and whoever is tapped on the word "blood" names a color which is spelled out, i.e., Red, "R-E-D and you are out." Each letter and the words "...and you are out," count as additional taps.

Along the same lines:

The sky is blue.
How old are you?

Then there is the lovely quatrain --

Engine, engine, number nine,
Going down the railroad line.
If the train should jump the railroad tracks,
Do you want your money back?

The answer (yes or no) is spelled out and the closing phrase "...and you are out," is repeated.

Eeny, Meani, Miny, Mo

This is similar to One Potato, Two Potato, except that the person recites:

Eeny, meani, miny, mo
Catch a tiger by the toe,
If he hollers, let him go,
My mother says you are out.

The caller points to each person on each word of the poem until "out" lands on one individual who is thus eliminated. The poem is repeated until one player remains.

There are many variations on the first three lines of the quatrain, though "mother" seems prevalent in all closing statements (preceding the final ouster -- OUT!) One clear exception, shy of any Shakespearean sonnet, is the quaint lyric:

Ink a bink a bottle of ink,
The cork fell out and you stink.
Not because you're dirty;
Not because you're clean;
Just because you kissed a (boy or) girl
Behind a magazine.

Tag

ORIGIN:

In pre-historic times, Tag was the creme-de-la-creme of recreation for religious buffs. Evil spirits lurking behind every corner sufficiently answered, "What makes megalithic Sammy run?" With only clubs for protection, they had no time to run away when they believed a host of spiritual beasties, plagues, and mastedons were chasing them. Before the days of therapy, penicillin, and the couch, the cave men believed their only safeguard and solace were in touching an object made of wood or stone to relieve their anxieties.

In some ancient games, breaking evil spells was as important as receiving immunity from the spirits which cast them. Today's sport is a far cry from fleeing death, evil spirits, and contagion (though that's hard to believe when watching the game), but the fundamentals remain, where one touch from a finger spreads the evil of being "it."

OBJECT:

To flee the evil touch of "it" and remain running free.

Tree chase.

One person is it the other poeple run a round and try to touch the bases. The trees are the bases. If your tagged and your not on the base your it. As many poeple you want can play.

8 yrs old

St. Louis, Mo.

RULES:

In simple "old-fashioned" Tag someone belts out, "Let's play Tag!" after which the spontaneous chain reaction of "Not it, not it, not it," follows, until the last domino to speak is -- "it!" Then the chasing begins with "it" madly racing after old friends, who euphemistically run for their lives. One touch, or tag, from the chaser and zap -- the game makes him "it".

A smart chaser often pretends to be tired, luring the prey in, and lashing out at the decisive moment. It is an unwise practice for a player to immediately tag "it" back once "it" has tagged him. This tends to rub tagsters the wrong way, resembling Idiot's Tag, "Gotcha last."

In Oklahoma, "it" runs around the house in circles (which might be hours) until he is tagged in the game called Tap the Icebox. In some areas, the newly tagged players join forces with "it" in proliferating evil, rather than being called out, or the new "it." Strangely, in some other areas, the one boy in the neighborhood wearing glasses often ends up being "it." There always comes a time, though, when "it" tags a hefty, stupid klunk, whose name is prefixed with "Big" or suffixed with an "o." The game usually ends in argument, exhaustion, or a nosebleed.

VARIATIONS:

Floating

The only safety from the impending doom of Tag is to be anywhere but on the ground. Clinging to a lamppost or tree limg is not unusual, particularly for players who are used to sleeping with a Teddy bear. For the casual passerby, this public display of affection for inanimate objects is bewildering. The player in Floating, however, finds his haven.

Touch

The oldest form of Touch is *Iron Tag*. Iron has had a superstitious association with good luck since the Middle Ages, evolving even to the good fortune attributed to the iron horseshoe above a home's doorway indicating the house was sure to be in good, reverent hands.

Whether iron, wood, cloth, or glass, however, all players in contact with a specified material (which housed protective powers) were not vulnerable to the touch of "it." Today many themes are used, such as color, where anything painted or inherently the specified color, is as good as gold.

Chain Tag

Anyone tagged becomes another "it" until the "its" overcome the community of survivors. The only escape is to "join 'em" and multiply. The last person left resigns himself to majority rule. Actually, any variation can be played with a chain reaction to speed the game to quick and definitive conclusion.

Run Down

*When you run the man got to tag you
Its two enders when the man count to ten you
got to run.
When he tag you your out,
When the runner get ten then he gets
a end.*

Roy Frank

Doctor Tag

The clear relationship between symptom and cause connects more obviously the chaser to the disease he carries in Doctor Tag. "It" touches a spot on the runner's body, and that area is beset with paralysis. If an arm is touched, the player must hold his plagued arm with his opposite hand. If a leg is hit by the disease, then it must be held by the victim's free hand. When paralysis hits one leg and Jonas Salk is on vacation, the player must hop away from "it" until help arrives. Two or three blows in the right places and the attacked player is as good as dead, there being no immunizations against "it." An ailing victim can only be relieved through the touch of a healthy individual who is unafraid to mingle with the sick. However, the healthy are unlikely to make house calls, since the closer the healthy get to the victim, the greater the likelihood that "it" will inflict his sting.

Freeze Tag

The game often called Stuck, Seven-eleven, etc., freezes solid all victims touched by "it" until thawed by a hot and free ally, a ploy which is used by a wise "it" to lure unfrozen runners into his territory. The object is for "it" to make Madame Tussaud's House of Wax seem like child's play. The real pro must put all the players into a deep freeze in order to win the game.

Elephant

Freeze Tag, a touch of calisthenics, and strong legs make up the body of Elephant Tag. Once tagged, a player remains frozen with his legs spread wide apart. The only way he can be released from bondage is when another free player crawls between his legs. If a player is tagged three times, he becomes "it."

Whaco

This variation brings weaponry to the lethal arsenal of "it." The chaser has a rope, shoe, stick, or towel with which to tag or hit his victims. This is one game where there is little debate on whether or not someone is tagged.

Along the coastal shores, snapping a towel is a favorite attack, while sticks, 2x4's, and shoes fare well inland.

Spider, Bike, or Piggy Back

All three games simply vary the means of locomotion of those being chased. In Spider Tag, everyone walks around on all fours, body facing upward as in Crab Soccer. In Bike or Piggy Back, the players ride their bikes and, in the latter, the backs of their friends while fleeing "it."

Shadow Tag

Sunny days are *a priori* for this game of Tag. "It" must tag someone's shadow rather than his actual being or flesh. The player's only escape to safety is to eclipse the sun and thus make his shadow disappear. Making friends with one's shadow, a thorough knowledge of trigonometry, and the secret of Stonehenge may help to make escape relatively easy -- especially at noon. But, in the late afternoon, it means searching for shade, the midnight sun, the aurora borealis -- or another game. Peter Pan had no difficulty escaping in Shadow Tag -- until Wendy came along.

Flashlight Tag

The antithesis of Shadow Tag, this game must be played in shade or darkness. Ever since the first flashlight was made in 1895, the game has risen to new heights, particularly with the invention of the battery. The very first (and cumbersome) flashlight weighed ten pounds which, without a dolly for wheeling purposes, made the game somewhat impractical. With the revised standard edition, "it" has only to zap a wanderer in the dark with a beam of light, and thus convert the wanderer into an "it." Like fireflies, the players blink their lights in the darkness of the playing field.

The game is most popular in the late summer, when the sun sets earlier and the evening air is still warm.

Balls and
Ball Bouncing

ORIGIN:

Playing with a ball is probably the earliest sport or game known today. Prehistoric man played throwing games with sticks or animal bones. Women playing ball were depicted in Egyptian murals as early as 2050 B.C. Not only is it the oldest sport known, but it is also the most universally found around the globe. Even barbaric tribes living on remote islands in the Indian Ocean were found playing ball by early explorers.

The Eskimos made balls of leather filled with moss, the Romans had pigskin ones inflated with air, people of the East Indies made them from bamboo, and the Americans invented the rubber pinky. The pinky or spaldeen, in fact, is the center of a tennis ball which was rejected for not meeting tennis-ball specifications.

The pinky is best known along the east coast, where approximately 12,000 gross are sold each year in the local candy stores. (The balls are seasonal and go dead relatively quickly.) Since they were first manufactured by A. G. Spalding around 1920, the balls have been used for packing and shipping on aircraft as well as for the standard summer city games.

OBJECT:

To catch and throw the ball. If that's tedious, a variety of chants are spoken or sung while bouncing the ball in rhythm. There are basically three types of games, and they require one ball and one player.

In type I called Wonderball, the player throws the ball straight up into the air and claps his hands as many times as he can before catching the descending ball.

The second kind involves bouncing the ball and throwing one's leg over the ball before it hits the ground on a certain beat of a chant (see page 32).

The final type of game (Mimsy) incorporates a chant with a series of corresponding gymnastics.

strawberry shortcake cream on top tell me the name of your sweetheart capital A, B,

Concentration

Composition letter *A*.
May I repeat the letter *A*,
Because I like the letter *A*?
Angie begins with the letter *A*.

Composition letter B
May I repeat the letter *B*,
Because I like the letter *B*?
Betsy begins with the letter B.

Concentration—the player bounces the ball on every *A* and goes on through the alphabet, B's, C's, etc., until a beat or ball is missed.

Indians playing with balls.

Mississippi

Miss-iss-ipp-i

Mississippi—on each *i* the ball is bounced.

Hello

<u>Hello</u>, Hello, <u>Hello</u>, Sir
Meet me at the <u>Grocer</u>

Hello—the ball is bounced on the underlined words.

A, My Name Is

(biographical sketch)

A, my name is Alice,
My husband's name is Albert,
And we come from Alabama,
And we sell apples

A, My Name Is—the player fills in his name, spouse's name, address, and occupation for each letter of the alphabet until he can't think of a name or misses the beat. The leg goes over the ball on each piece of new information.

O'Leary

One, two, three O'Leary,
My first name is Mary.
If you think it's necessary,
Look it up in the dictionary.
One, two, three O'Leary,
My first name is Jerry.
Don't you think I look cute
In my mother's bathing suit?

O'Leary—the player's leg goes ove
the ball on each O'Leary and eac
word that ends phonetically wit
ary. On the last word of each verse
the player throws the ball into th
air and catches it with both hand
if and when it returns.

+ "Wall Ball"
— bouncing a ball at an angle on the ground so it hit the wall and then catching it —
Yours Sincerely,

Angela Lansbury

Type III - Mimsy
A mimsy,
A clapsie,
I roll my hands,
Touch backsie.
My right hand,
My left hand,
High as the sky,
Low as the sea.
I touch my knee,
And my heel,
And my toe,
And over we go.
(Keep going until player falls apart.)

Mimsy Directions
Throw the ball to ground.
Clap hands.
Gesture hands in circular motion.
Touch back with both hands.
Touch back with right hand.
Touch back with left hand.
Both hands above head.
Touch the ground.
Touch knee.
Touch heel.
Touch toe.
Bounce ball under leg.
(Each feat is done between ball bounces.)

Ancient Sicilian Mosaic of women playing ball.

Blindman's Bluff

ORIGIN:

Blindman's Bluff is a game of literary note in the English language. It is often mentioned in novels, short stories, and plays. In its very earliest form, two thousand years ago, it was the popular sport of Greek boys who called it Muinda, or Brazen Fly. While one boy was blindfolded, his gentle playmates whipped him with papyrus husks until one of them was caught. The Greek game may have even been derived earlier from rites of human sacrifice in pre-historic religions of man.

Elizabethans took a kinder approach and smacked the hooded victim with a knotted hood or rope, very much like snapping a towel at a blind person. Later, fondling replaced hitting, and the game hit an all-time high for court foreplay and jest. After fondling led to mufky-pufky and other assorted *rites de massage,* the Victorians put an end to such sensory gestures. Today's version, declining in popularity by the hour, is less violent and sexual. It is this higher degree of civilized playing that has actually led to its decline.

EQUIPMENT:

6 or more human beings
1 blindfold or scarf

From 14th century manuscript. (Hoodman's Blind)

18th Century painting by Goya.

OBJECTIVE:

One blindfolded person must catch and identify the people around him.

RULES:

One person is chosen to be blindfolded. Then comes the long ritual of checking out the blindfold. Once the scarf is tightly tied, the blinded player is subject to a series of questions such as: "How many fingers am I holding up?" or "What color is my shirt?" until everyone is convinced that the blindfolded person cannot see. After blindness is assured, the player is spun three or four times by his playmates just to insure his utter confusion. Meanwhile, all those who can see, circle around the blindman until he claps his hands three times, whereupon all movement stops. The blind man haphazardly points to someone on the circle. Then that chosen player must enter the circle, making noise and dodging his handicapped pursuer. Once caught by the blindman, however, he must submit to examination. The blindman can touch the player's clothes, face, or hair for purposes of identification. If the victim is identified, he becomes the next blindman.

Sometimes it is played with a bit less organization when the circle formation is eliminated. The blindman is spun to the point of dizziness while his fellow players dodge, sneer, and make noises behind his back. Even among friends, there is double-dealing, and one player won't hesitate to shove a friend into the blindman. Once someone is touched by the blindman, he is caught. There on in, the game follows its natural course.

Pebble (Filbert) Pitching

ORIGIN:

The Filbert is the European species of the American hazelnut. Filberts were known to the Chinese over 5,000 years ago, and there are records of filbert pitching with pebbles as far back as the ancient Greeks. The filbert nuts are grown in Yugoslavia, Italy, Spain, the United States, England, and many other countries today (though "How often do you play with filbert nuts?" is a question not likely to be too often asked). The actual game is best known to the American Jewish people around the time of Passover and in some parts of the country, Rosh Hashana as well. This holiday game quickly fades into Johnny on a Pony, Stickball, and Tag with the advent of spring and summer.

EQUIPMENT:
1 bag of filberts
a piece of chalk

OBJECT:
   To get the filberts in a hole or roll the nuts as close to the curb without hitting it.

RULES:

Part One

   In ancient times, pebbles were thrown into shallow holes from a point three feet from a hole. Today each player has one nut and one turn to throw the filbert as close to the curb as he can without hitting it. Usually it is thrown or rolled from a point six feet from the curb. Whoever gets closest goes first in the second part of the game. Everyone else goes in the order of the proximity of their nuts to the curb. The first part of the game, which decides the playing order, is perhaps the most crucial step toward a final victory.

Part Two

   A chalk line is drawn three feet from a hole where the gutter meets the curb. It doesn't take long to find a hole along the edge of the street. Each player gives his nut to the person going first, who shoots them all at the hole. Every nut that goes in, he keeps. The remaining nuts go to the second player. The game goes down the line of players in the same manner until there are no nuts to be had. This is the sad disadvantage to those who blew their shot in the first part of the game.
   Obviously, those who didn't get a chance to shoot their nuts are not in the running, and the chances of being eliminated grow greater with each turn. These outcasts must practice with their nuts until the game swings back into vogue the following spring. Success in both parts of the game is essential for final victory. One helpful pointer: Watch your nuts carefully between matches and be careful not to crack them.
   Whoever has the most nuts wins the match.

Cluster of four filbert nuts

Street Hockey

Ancient Greek bas-relief.

ORIGIN:

Street Hockey is a cross between Ice and Field Hockey. Field Hockey, one of the oldest games in existence today, was played by the Aztecs and most North American Indian tribes. Artistically depicted in all corners of the world, Hockey has spanned the centuries -- from a woodcut of ancient Greece in 5 A.D., to a Danish dish depicting two men "bulling off" a ball, to a modern painting of Indians starting the game.

It was not until 1875 that the English officially codified the sport, first as Bandy and later as Hockey. The name Hockey was probably derived from the French *hocquet,* which means a shepherd's crook similar to the hooked stick used in the game. Today, there are teams in many countries, but the Indians are the unrivaled champions of the world.

On the other hand, Ice Hockey is a relatively modern game evolved from the earlier field game. The games differ basically in that a puck replaces the ball, and the players shoot on ice instead of dirt. It was played in Holland in the mid-18th century. Two or three hundred years later and 3,500 miles across the Atlantic in another land of icy ponds, the first club was organized in Canada. After the rules were officially set up in Montreal , a Canadian student introduced the game to the United States at Johns-Hopkins University in the late 19th century. Some consider the game an icy, civilized form of Lacrosse, but that was before Hockey took to the streets.

EQUIPMENT:

Hockey sticks (15-inch blades)
1 puck (a small ½-to-1 inch thick piece of cylindrical rubber)
Chalk (optional)
Roller skates (optional)

OBJECT:

For each competing team to knock the puck through its opponent's goal.

RULES:

Street Hockey uses the stick as in the Field game, but most of the other aspects of the game are closer to Ice Hockey. The street parallels the ice; the curb, the rink; roller skates give the mobility of ice skates -- and last, but not least, fist fights parallel with fist fights. All the rules of Ice Hockey apply.

Two center players stand facing each other with the puck between them. They hit the ground and then each other's stick three times before the puck is hit into play. Each man tries to smash the puck into his own territory (called "bulling off"). The team with the puck passes it among themselves via swats of the stick. The team moves the puck down the street toward the goal of the other side, while some of the team players remain behind to guard their goal should the puck reverse directions. Guarding each goal is one player who throws his whole body between the oncoming team and the goal. Some goalies, by size alone, can cover quite a bit of territory.

```
        we'd wait to catch our best buddy against the

curb and go sailing into him.  He'd go flying across the

sidewalk and climb up one of the gardens of the semi-detached

houses that fronted most of the block on Crown Street between

Albany and Kingston where I lived the biggest part of my

adolescence.

                              Sincerely,

                              Norman Mailer
                              Norman Mailer
```

Any puck under a car is out of bounds (and often out of reach). Whenever the puck leaves the rink, it is played from that spot. Frequently, time is called for no other reason than a player's belief that disruption of play and a little more time will aid his ailing team.

Constant disruption often leads to the total disruption of the game. Once the brawl begins, the real excitement starts. The shrill of skates on asphalt, foul language, cursing, fist and stick fights -- all add little to the tranquility of the neighborhood, but there's a lot of tension released. Even the common cheer captures the physical brutality of the game:

> *Ahl-a-man, ahl-a-man*
> *Diego, San Diego*
> *Ish Kish, pish kish*
> *Hit him in the kishkers. Yea Team!*

SCORING:

One point is scored every time the puck goes past the goalie and into the goal. The goalie can stop, pick up, and throw the puck back into play to save the point if it doesn't go past him. (If a member sends the puck through his *own* goal, he is also sent through the goal by his teammates since the point goes to the opposing team.) Providing there are any survivors, the team with any men left (as well as the highest number of points) wins.

My street games in Houston, Texas were roller hockey and bicycle polo, but unfortunately I don't believe there are any photographs that caught me as I starred in these pursuits. Sorry.

Sincerely yours,

Walter Cronkite

Cat's Cradle

ORIGIN:

The game is of Asiatic origin. Starting in China thousands of years ago, string-figures passed westward along early trade routes. The game in itself is a map of man's early migration. It has been found among savages and civilized men alike. Wherever there is an inordinate amount of time to kill, the amusement is most prevalent. The Eskimos, for example, living in the land of the midnight sun, have invented the most intricate string patterns known on earth. Beside passing time, the

Eskimos have infused the cradle with their own myths. When the sun sets to the south in the fall, the game is played, symbolically capturing the sun in the meshings of the string in order to prevent it from disappearing.

Symbolically, to the English, it represents four leashed dogs, while to the Cherokee Indians, it's a set of crow's feet. However, the most common name and symbol for the game is Cat's Cradle (cratch cradle), derived from the archaic definition of the word "cratch," which means manger. In Britain today, the word is defined as crib or frame, describing the string figure more accurately as the "frame of a cradle."

Many cradles require two sets of hands, but there are many designs, such as the witch's hat, butterfly, and Jacob's ladder which can be done by an individual. Some of the games even involve using one's feet and teeth.

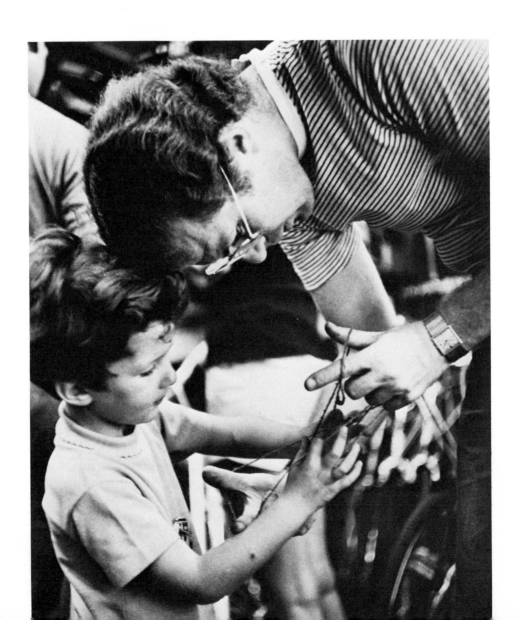

Below are some drawings and pictures of the more common patterns. Directions have been left out since written explanation would only tangle the reader in words and require in itself a complete volume on making string-figures.

Hide and Seek

All hid, all hid:
an old infant play

"Love's Labours Lost"—Shakespeare
IV. iii. 78.

ORIGIN:

Hide and Seek, commonly found in literature throughout history, was well known to the Greeks as *Apodidraskinda* at least three hundred years before the birth of Christ. In ancient times, Hide and Seek, or "Running Home," was played very much as it is today. One player closed his eyes while the others ran off to secret hiding places. Then, as the seeker went on his hunt, one of his camouflaged compatriots tried to return to home base, unnoticed, to become the next seeker.

In Greece, the coveted role belonged to the seeker, unlike today's game, in which there are many other variations and complications added onto the ancient Running Home. Yet they all fall into three basic forms -- all seek one, one seek all, and all race home while being sought. The names and themes often reflect the times and romance of a given culture. The United States has run the gamut. During the Buck Rogers-Flash Gordon days, Martians versus the Earthlings was big. Terry and the Pirates inspired Captains versus the Pirates. Cowboys and Indians were strong during the Cisco Kid, Pancho, Gene Autry, "Happy Trails To You," and Hopalong Cassidy popularity. Cops and Robbers came about with Dillinger, Bogart, Dragnet, and the immortalizing of Bonnie and Clyde. James Bond -- 007 -- gave rise to Spy versus Spy (with spy kits included), while Man from U.N.C.L.E. made the game Superheroes versus Supervillains. The kinky paraphernalia, secret codes, fantasies, and romance run through the heart of all Hide and Seek games.

The great author of "Kidnapped," "Treasure Island," and countless other stories, Robert Louis Stevenson, recognized the limitless adventure, mystery, and intrigue conjured in the Hide and Seek mind of youthful fantasy.

I loved hide and seek. We'd start with Make a Circle in the old man's back. You had about ten seconds to guess who punched you in the back if you didn't want to be 'it'. The 'it' hid and the rest of us raced back to the lamppost before 'it', once we were seen. Those who really had guts were the farthest away from the post. Once you made a safe landing you shouted "Olie, olie in free." This was my favorite game when I was about six or seven years old.

Rod Serling

---

46   Street Games

OBJECTIVE:

For one or more players to seek those in hiding.

Cops and Robbers
The games I play are very
simple. The game is called Cops and Robbers. We pick two teams. One team is
the cops and the others the robbers. The
robbers hide and the cops find them. When the
cops find them they have to tag the robbers.
After they tag some the rest of the robbers and
free the ones that are caught. After the robbers are all caught its the cops turn to be
robbers you keep on switching.

Jimmie
Age 11 S.F. CA.

RULES:

Appealing to a basic human urge, noted early in the Bible, "Seek and Ye shall find," the rules of the game have survived the years incorporating fair and unfair play. Again, this will reflect a particular culture at a particular point in time.

Most commonly, someone everyone generally feels is the most "common" ends up being picked as the seeker, or "it." And very often the game starts and repeats with the very same person ("it") going to his corner, lamppost, or home base to count off. As "it" counts off to 100, everyone else flees to an inconvenient hiding place. For some strange reason, the count-down is merely a second or two longer than the one in Red Light-Green Light (see page 231), which is a count from one-to-ten. (There are cases where the seeker can't count to a hundred, so it's ten times all ten fingers, or, more recently, counting to twelve-base-eight, with his eyes shut.)

As the count-down (or up) ends, most of the hiders are far away, tucked behind a pile of dirty newspapers, lying low in a service entrance, or well cramped in a garbage pail. The seeker declares, "Here I come, ready or not," a threat bearing little impact on anyone, and the search begins. Anyone spotted by "it" must come out of hiding. The denouement of the game is reached when either everyone has been found or the first person spotted reaches home base, proclaiming, "Oly, oly—home free," before the seeker finds any of the players. Should everyone reach the base safely, a new game begins with the seeker seeking again. At the end of a long game or day, the group heads for home, though there is probably at least one zealous friend who is so well hidden (or several miles away) that the game is long over before he comes out of hiding.

VARIATIONS:

I Spy

The spy or "it" counts to the usual hundred and sets off to find those hiding. Once he spots a player, he rushes back to home base (or spy headquarters) and yells, "one, two, three" and the name of the spotted player. Once a player realizes he's been found, he races the spy back to home base in an effort to yell his own "one, two, three," naming himself. If he beats the spy out, he's safe.

Should the spy get to headquarters first and miscalculate, incorrectly naming the person he spotted, both the named and the person found are free to go back into hiding.

During the game, any player can make a self-sacrificing run for home base to outrun the spy, bringing himself safely "in from the cold." However, anyone caught or correctly named by the spy becomes the new spy in the next game. This is best played at night, when the darkness cloaks the war with atmosphere and poor visibility.

Relievio or Ring-a-lievio

First, a five- or six-foot square is drawn and designated the den or prison. Second, everyone is chosen to be on one of two teams. One of the teams then runs away from the den and hides. When the captain of the hiding team yells, "ready," the other team sets out to hunt down the members of the opposition.

Once a player is spotted, the seeker must hold onto his caught victim and say, "Caught, caught, caught," to insure capture. In this brief encounter the sport of Relievio is revealed. The victim wiggles, pulls, and fights back, while a seeker clutches onto him during the vigorous (and often violent) confrontation. If the victim is captured, he is led to the den as a prisoner, and the seeker heads out to find new prey.

One member of the seeker's team always remains to guard the den. Any courageous player from the opposing team can come out of hiding, run through the den shouting, "Ring-a-lievio -- one, two three," to free one prisoner. Only one prisoner can be freed at a time. If the denkeeper catches the daring saviour or fleeing escapee, the latter lose their short-lived freedom. After a specified time limit has passed, the teams switch roles. The team that accumulates the most prisoners at the end of the match wins.

The kids game I remember most vividly was "ring-a-leavio" played in Red Hook, Little Italy Brooklyn in the early 1920's — ... Two teams, one home base — anyone captured on the free team was incarcerated in a chalk circle home-base — he could be freed only by a raid on the circle ... the liberator, untagged could free the captive or captives — sides changed when all were captured ... of course there were geographic limits, + team captains had to rely on honesty of their team — I hope this helps you. Good luck on the book
sincerely – Eli Wallach

ELI WALLACH

SARDINES

One player is chosen to be "it," who, in this variation, is the sought rather than the seeker. "It" goes out to hide, while all the other players stick around home base, mumbling in unison to a hundred with their eyes closed. If a passer-by didn't know any better, he would think they were praying.

Once the lucky number 100 has been reached, each player ventures out in his own direction after "it." Once a seeker discovers "it," he must take refuge with "it" without his teammates noticing. Each seeker, upon his discovery, joins the party. If it gets too crowded after several dozen seekers have pushed their way into the hiding quarters of "it," where there is no more room, even for air, the later arrivals must sit near their discovery, in plain view of their remaining teammates. This should indicate to their teammates that the goldmine is nearby (but may still be hard to find without some clever digging). More often than not, all the players squeeze together, packed in like sardines, compressing "it" into a fossil.

Ten Steps

This game is the same as I Spy, except for the opening count and the limitation of how far the hiders can go.

At the outset, it's a bit like Red Light-Green Light (see page 231). "It," with his back to the scattering hiders, counts to ten, turning around on the tenth count. On that final count, all the runners must freeze where they are. If "it" sees any hider moving, he must come back to home base and start over again. "It" repeats the count five times, following the same procedure.

Any player still in the visual range of the seeker by the fifth count, becomes the new "it." The retired seeker watches the game -- or heads down the road for an ice cream. When everyone is out of sight, or there is a new "it," by the fifth count, the game proceeds as I Spy from that point on.

Drop the Handkerchief

ORIGIN:

Looking back to ancient Greece, *Schoenophilinda* shines through the centuries, closely paralleling the English pastime, Whackem. Young children all over the world play the game today, though it's a bit more popular in the British Isles.

OBJECTIVE:

In this racing game, the tagger races against the "tagee" for the tagged person's spot in a circle.

EQUIPMENT:

12 or more human beings
1 handkerchief or rag

RULES:

Everyone in the group holds hands and forms a circle, except the one person chosen "it." All the members of the circle release each other's hands and remain standing or sitting in that spot. "It" walks around the outside of the circle carrying the handkerchief, while the group sings:

I sent a letter to my love,
And on the way I dropped it.
One of you has picked it up
And put it in your pocket.

At some point in the song or walk, "it" drops the handkerchief behind one of the players. The handkerchief falls, the die is cast. Once that realization strikes, the player whips out of the circle and races around, in the opposite direction from that taken by the dropper, in an effort to get back to his own spot before "it" does.

Each player can judge how badly off he is in the race by where they pass each other in relation to the empty spot. Usually, the dropper gets there first. But in either case, the last one back is "it" and must drop the handkerchief

next. Players in the circle are not supposed to watch the outside runner nor look behind them until the runner has passed.

The game can be played as a chase as well as a race. In a chase, the runner picked and "it" run in the same direction. If "it" is tagged by the chaser, then "it" must go again until he reaches an empty spot without being tagged.

VARIATIONS:

There are many ways to play this game, but the essential difference is in what object other than a handkerchief is used and how it is administered to the circle. It varies from tapping with the hands to slamming someone over the head with a stick.

An example of the more gentle tapping type is Duck, Duck, Goose. The runner goes racing around tapping each member on the head. With each tap, he says "Duck," but when someone is knighted "Goose," the race is on as in Drop the Handkerchief.

In one rural part of the country, capitalists and communists were substituted for duck and goose. In a few urban areas, duck and goose were dropped altogether in favor of a pure sensory experience. The impact of the tap would determine who was chosen. One good whack on the head and that person was --"Goose."

Another chant used in Drop the Handkerchief:

A tisket, a tasket,
A green and yellow basket.
I wrote a letter to my love,
And on the way I dropped it.
And one of you has picked it up,
And put it in your pocket.
It isn't you -- it isn't you ...

*repeats until the handkerchief is dropped -- and then *it's you!*

Knuckles or Knucks

ORIGIN:

The origin is not exactly known. However, it was probably played in pre-historic times. The only equipment needed in the earlier form of the game was a set of knuckles, and they were readily available even to Cro-Magnon man. Later, the invention of cards refined the game which is found in most countries around the world today.

EQUIPMENT:

2 hands
1 deck of cards

OBJECTIVE:

To test physical endurance and pain tolerance.

RULES:

There seems to be no other reason to play Knuckles except to draw blood, and that requires very little reason. Before the blood bath begins, most often the participants play Poker, Casino, Rummy 500, or the like, to determine who will be knuckled. Yet others do not bother with such preliminaries and get right down to it.

One of the two players holds his arm out straight, clenches his fist, and bares his knuckles. The other combatant strikes a mighty blow to his opponent. This knuckle-to-knuckle combat alternates between hitting and being hit. Within minutes the shots are more powerful and fierce in an effort to knuckle in the opponent before he has a chance to smash back. Each player relishes the anguish he incurs. The ideals of bravery, the suffering servant, "Taking your medicine...," a good soldier, martyrdom, can't be truly enjoyed without suffering substantial pain.

In some African tribes, boys reaching puberty are circumcised with slices of bamboo. Without anesthetic, each tribe member endures the pain bravely, heralding his *rites de passage* to manhood. Knuckles, perhaps, satisfies this need of ritual in American youth. This game, not unlike circumcision, even removes a piece or two of skin, draws blood, and hurts. However, in Knuckles, both sexes play and one bleeding victim must surrender in defeat to end the game. Those who watch the game view it as a Roman blood bath in the Coliseum, where defeat is dishonorable. But, two stubborn, proud players, sprinkled with a touch of Vlad the Impaler, wooed by a Joan-of-Arc syndrome, will play the game to the bloody end. The game appeals to the very heart of what good sense finds appalling.

VARIATIONS:

Knuckles played with a deck of cards is a cut and dry revision. One player holds a deck of cards tightly between the inside of his thumb and forefinger. He smashes the deck down on his opponent's knuckle, ensuring pain, blood, and grafting. Either one's pride or hand is damaged. Most players seem to prefer the physical agony rather than the disgrace.

When the game is preceded by a hand of Poker or Gin, the winner executes the knuckling of his choice.

LINGO:

Hard -- slamming the deck onto the hand as hard as possible.

Soft -- a light tap with the deck.

Scrape -- pulling the edge of the deck slowly across the knuckles.

Sandwich -- the victim places his hand between the cards, 26 on the bottom and 26 on the top. The hitter smacks down his fists on the cards sandwiching his opponent's wedged hand.

Nuggie -- two knuckles delivered to the skull (used on special occasions).

Guillotine -- a center portion of the deck is raised one inch above the pack. Then the loaded deck is placed in position and the executioner fires a blow to the raised portion.

  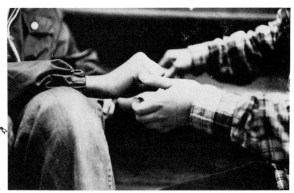

Left to Right : Guillotine,
Sandwich,
Scrape

EQUIVALENCY CHART (Alternatives)

5 softs equal 1 hard
2 hards equal 1 scrape
2 scrapes equal 1 guillotine
3 hards equal 1 sandwich

In the long run, cards hold up better than knuckles. This version ends earlier in embarrassment, pain, foul language, or tears than the knuckle-to-knuckle combat.

Dodgeball

OBJECTIVE:

For one or more players to put out the surrounding players by hitting them with a fly ball.

ORIGIN:

Dodgeball as we know it today has three basic formulas: one team against another, every man for himself, and circle dodge. All the early simple forms of Dodgeball combined an element of these three games.

Ostrakinda, or the shell game played in ancient Greece, unified the seemingly impossible task of every man for himself and team work -- all under one roof. A white shell was darkened on one side. Then the Greeks divided themselves into two teams, black or white, night or day. The shell was given a spin and the shell side which turned up was the chasing team. Each time the shell was spun, the roles reversed, and role-changing was frequent in Ostrakinda. Plato paralleled the game with love. The lover once pursued becomes the pursuer and tries to capture his lover who is running away; as with the "shell being turned again" in the normal course of the game, the roles reverse. This was the forerunner of the Elizabethan Court Dodge, though Shakespeare did not find an easy way to liken it to love. The game is still played in Greece and a dozen Mediterranean and Eastern countries as Day and Night or Black and White.

Two other games, not quite as old as Black and White, are Ball-he and Kingy. The United States inherited them from the English colonists, who fostered what is commonly known today as Dodgeball or Fudge in parts of the Midwest.

EQUIPMENT:

1 large ball or
tennis ball (tennis ball stings more)
a good game requires at least 10 or 15 players

RULES:

(Himself:)

This is the least formal version of the game. It is the most often played because it's easy to set up since there is nothing to set up. It is most desirable on a day when "there is nothing to do" and no one wants to "do anything."

One person is chosen "it" and counts to ten while everyone else scatters. He then pursues those around him by bouncing or dribbling the ball. The other players dodge the oncoming ball which approaches them at 50 M.P.H. when thrown full force by a teen-ager. Any target between the head and toes is fair play. Unless the ball is caught upon impact, the player is out. The last survivor is crowned king, who chooses who will be "it" next.

For added adventure and chaos, there is the variation Multiplication Dodge, in which each person hit with the ball becomes another "it." Your friendly neighbor suddenly becomes "it," turns on *you*, and rams the ball down *your* throat. The only way to stop the proliferation of "its" is for a non-"it" to catch the ball, putting the "it" who threw it at him out of commission. The battle continues until one alert player is left who is not an "it." He is declared the winner.

If one feels persecuted, he will be happy in this game because everyone is out to get him. To make matters and paranoia worse, some variations include a "freeze" clause. The original "it," after counting to ten, calls "freeze" -- and every player must remain motionless in his tracks. Though "it" cannot dribble the ball, as the number of "its" increase, the odds stack up in his favor, leaving non-"its" fairly helpless. The vibrant and kinetic game of Multiplication Dodge converts players into cowering sitting ducks lashing out at each other when the right moment strikes.

Every Man for

Team:

Two teams are chosen up and each goes to the opposite side of a drawn center line. No member from one team can cross into the other team's zone. If a player happens to be close to the center line when the other team gets the ball, he's had it. Though there is better hitting power up close there is equally as much danger when the ball comes whirling back. Anyone hit with the ball is out, and anyone who catches the ball on a fly puts out the thrower. Team members can pass the ball among themselves as long as it does not touch the ground. Should the ball hit the ground, it is forfeited to the other team. This is the only friendly moment between teams. The team obliterated first, loses.

Circle

This, like the former game, has two teams. One team forms a large circle enclosing the other team, the members of which are scattered about inside. Members of the circle try to hit the players inside, who can dodge the ball in any way they know how without leaving the circle. Anyone hit becomes part of the man-hitting circle until no one is left inside.

In a slight variation, retaliatory power is given to the dodgers. If they catch the ball, the circle member must join the dodge corps against the surrounding strike force. The balance of players between the inside of the circle and the circle itself shifts often, making this game never-ending.

Tug of War

OBJECTIVE:

One team must pull the other team or a mark on the rope over a designated line.

ORIGIN:

The game is not as popular today as it was during the Elizabethan era or even Hellenic Greece. In Greece, it was known as *Dielkustinda* and suggested earlier religious rites. The Tug of War might have symbolized a holy war between the sacred and the profane. The Druids, or even earlier cultures, often fused primitive religion and play into symbolic games such as Tug of War and Tag.

EQUIPMENT:

1 long unknotted rope (The professionals like to use a rope 35 feet long.)
8 or more humans (the heftier the better)

WORLD RECORDS
Largest rope: 48 inches in diameter, 3,780 yards in length. Used for the British liner Great Eastern.
Longest rope: Made in 1868 and was 10,000 fathoms or 59,980.9 feet long.

RULES:

The group is divided into two equal teams, at least numerically equal. One person on each team is chosen as the anchor man. The strongest, meanest, and heaviest person makes the best choice for this coveted position. Some might debate whether or not the anchor is a person.

Regardless of philosophies, the anchor puts the rope under his arm and over his shoulder or ties it around his waist. The rest of the tuggers align themselves along the rope and take it in their hands with a firm grip. When the "go" signal is sounded, each team tries to pull the opposing team over the center line. There is nothing theological about it today -- brute strength is what counts.

In *London Bridge,* a variation, all the players form a human rope and tug by putting their arms around each other and pulling. The most common word heard during this game is not "amen" but "heave." The anchorman's jolly command, "heave," signals his team to make one hard and heavy thrust backward to knock the opposing team off-balance. Each call of "heave" is followed by a group groan until one team moans and loses. More often than not, one team loses by fagging out rather than the other team winning by strength and force. This is evident when one team suddenly collapses and lets go of the rope, while the tugging, heaving side propels backward, plummeting to the ground (or into a parked car). Often the victorious team is anxious to rechallenge the losers -- just so they can get their shot at letting go of the rope.

Monkey In The Middle

ORIGIN:

The Greeks were playing *Chytrinda* around 200 A.D., a game in which one boy--the *chytra* (or pot)--sat down on the ground while the others hit, circled, badgered, and pinched him. If the pot caught one of them, he who was caught became the next pot in the middle. Later in Greece, another game called Sweet Wine followed the same format as Pot, except that the person in the middle had a knotted rope to hit his tormentors in retalliation, rather than just tagging them. This rope variation comes close to the American game Baste the Bear. However, *Chytrinda*, in its early form, most probably became the well-known European game, Frog in the Middle, in which the frog sits on the ground or remains on his knees.

The outside circle badgers the frog, singing, "Frog in the middle, can't catch me." The frog is never allowed to get off the ground while attempting to attack back, but if he tags someone from the circle, the "tagee" becomes the next frog. In America, the badgering remains, the circle is dropped, a ball is added, and the status of frog has been elevated to monkey, baboon -- or pickle. In some parts of the United States, the game is called Pickle in the Middle.

EQUIPMENT:

3 human beings (more resembles Keep Away)
1 rubber or tennis ball

OBJECTIVE:
To keep the ball away from the monkey.

RULES:
One of three people is picked to be the monkey. The other two zoo keepers stand twenty-to-thirty feet apart with the monkey midway between them. Then the zoo keepers have a catch with the ball. The idea is to throw the ball over the monkey's head. Once the ball leaves one of the zoo keeper's hands, the monkey can run anywhere between them to intercept the ball. This is a tiresome process because by the time the monkey arrives at one side, the ball is already on the way to the other. The keepers try to keep the ball away from the monkey, while jeering and wearing him out. Should the monkey catch the ball, whoever has thrown it becomes the next monkey, and if the monkey retrieves the ball, dropped by a keeper, the poor fumbler goes to the humiliating middle.

No one wants to be the monkey's uncle or anything closely related, but the game has survived 1500 years--rest in peace Charles Darwin.

VARIATION:

Ga-Ga
is actually an Israeli game, following the same principle as Monkey in the Middle, except that the ball is hit along the ground as if playing Slapball (see page 149) on one's knees.

Mumbly-peg (Jackknife)

ORIGIN:

Ever since megalithic man spent his days hunting for food and killing one another, the knife has been a mainstay of recreation The formalized game, however, didn't become overtly popular till pirates, who used knives for games (as well as each others' throats), landed on the English mainland in the early 1500's. In those good old days, the game required only two knife-throwing skills, frontsies and backsies (though it's not easy to imagine a pirate talking about "frontsies"). The two games were usually followed by the special ritual of the winner knocking a peg into the ground with his knife in as many blows as the loser took turns to complete the game. Then, in an act of humility, the loser proceeds to remove the peg with his teeth. Luckily, this ritual went out of style before the invention of dentures.

From a phonetic point of view, sitting face down into the ground, groveling over a peg, is not the best condition to demonstrate annunciation. Such mumbling orators gave rise to the game's name, "Mumble-peg," which was even mumbled and garbled further to Mumblety-peg. It is easier just to call it "Knifie."

EQUIPMENT:
    1 penknife

GENERAL RULES:

Courtesy of National Park and Recreation Association

Players must either sit or kneel on the ground. (Very Safe)

Best out of three long games or seven short games determines the winner.

Knife must stick into ground so that judge can get the thickness of at least two fingers between the ground and knife handle.

Boy Scout knife will be considered as official. (Very American)

Belt punch will be considered as the "blade."

To be done with right hand only except where indicated. (Very Right Hand Biased)

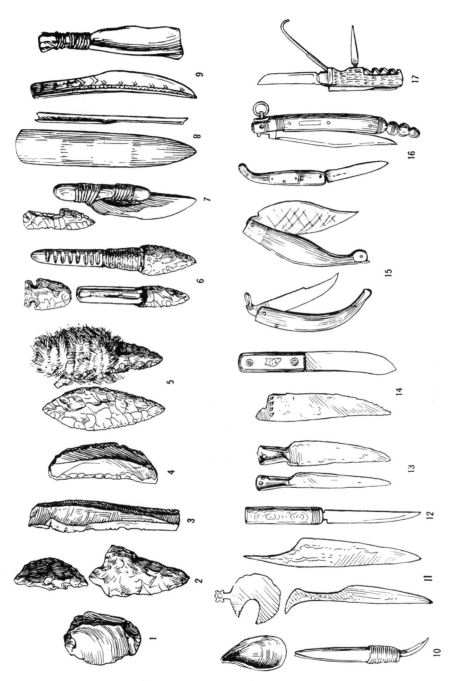

DEVELOPMENT OF JACKKNIFE.

WORLD RECORD
Penknife with Most Blades is the "Year" knife by Joseph Rodgers & Sons Ltd. who built it in 1882 with 1,882 blades and has continued adding on 1 blade for each year in the Christian Era until 2,000 A.D.

PENKNIFE RULES (ABRIDGED)

FRONT. — Knife on palm of right hand with blade toward finger tips; toss knife upward and inward, causing blade to stick in ground.

BACK. — Place knife on back of right hand and toss as for front.

PUNCH. — Make a fist with right hand. Place knife handle across the fingernails with blade toward thumb; twist hand quickly toward the left, sticking blade into the ground.

SNAPS. — Hold blade between thumb and forefinger of left hand with handle pointing toward the right. Strike the handle downward sharply with right hand, causing blade to stick into the ground. This must be done three times in succession.

SEVEN PENNIES. — Hold blade between thumb and first finger of right hand with handle away from contestant and snap knife away from tosser, sticking it into the ground. This must be done seven times in succession.

AROUND THE HORN. — Hold blade of knife between the index finger and thumb of right hand, as for **Pennies,** and swing the knife, with handle toward the ground, around the head from left to right; then snap away from tosser as in **Seven Pennies.**

SHAVE THE PEG. — Place blade between the first and second fingers and hold with thumb, have handle pointing away from body and point of blade toward person tossing; snap knife away from tosser.

CUT LEFT.—Hold knife as for **Pennies,** and snap downward across left arm, striking left wrist with the right.

CUT RIGHT.—Opposite to **Cut Left.**

As a boy I played the ordinary games, such as hide-and-seek, with other children. I also played a game called hockey or shinny, usually involving a tin can that had been smashed into about the size of a baseball, which was hit around by use of a home-made hockey stick, cut from the branch of a tree, with a bend in it. I also played jacks, sand-lot baseball (except that in Portland, Oregon, it might be called mud-lot baseball), and another game whose name I have forgotten. This game was played with a sharpened stick, about one and one-quarter inches in diameter and eighteen inches long. The game consisted in the first player's throwing the stick down into the clay soil, where it stood upright. The second player tried to throw his stick in such a way that it would hit the other stick and knock it down, while at the same time itself penetrating the soil and remaining standing.

Sincerely,

LINUS PAULING

J *a*
c *k*
s

Ancient knuckle-bones

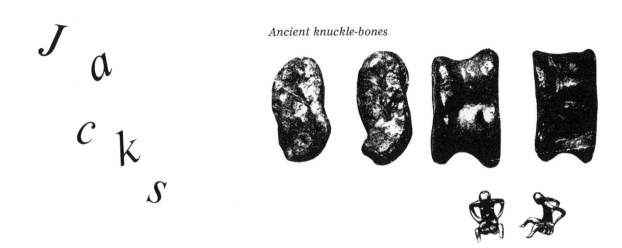

. . . and carved jackstones

ORIGIN:

Evidence of Knucklebones, the forerunner of Jacks and Jackstones, was first found in Kiev and attributed to pre-historic man. Surely the Greeks and Japanese played the game over 2,000 years ago, with little stones or bones. One player threw the bones up in the air and tried to catch as many of them as he could on the back of his hand as they descended. In France, local butchers still give children the bones of lambs to play the game with. Dried shoulder and vertebrae bones were most popular with early Americans -- even the Shakers played Jacks with pebbles during the warm months of the year. With the advent of steel, the six-pointed Jackstone was manufactured, and a red rubber ball was added to the game.

Ancient Greeks playing Knuckle-bone

Though the rules of the National Park and Recreation Association accurately describe the various games, the names have a less-formal tone among Jacks players. For example: One and Two—Onesies, Twosies; Back and Front—Backsies and Frontsies.

> My favorite of all the games was jacks. I was the champion of the entire block. Most probably because I had very large hands. They were the largest among all my friends in the neighborhood.
> *Charles Lindbergh*

JACKSTONES, WITH BALL

RULES (In all games no jackstones may be moved except those being played.)

Baby Game (Ones)

Scatter all jacks upon the playing surface by a single movement of the right hand. Toss the ball, pick up one jack, and after ball has bounced once, catch the ball in the same (right) hand. Transfer the jack to the left hand and proceed as before until all six jacks are in the left hand.

Twos

Jacks are picked up by twos; otherwise proceed as in Ones. Same for Threes, Fours (four and then two, or two then four), Fives (one and then five, or five then one), Sixes (all at once).

Downs And Ups

All jacks and ball in right hand. Toss ball upward, lay down all jacks, and catch ball in right hand. Throw ball up again, pick up all jacks, and catch ball in right hand.

Eggs In Basket

Scatter jacks, toss ball, pick up one jack. Right hand only used, and while ball bounces once, transfer jacks to the left hand, then catch ball in right hand. When all jacks have been picked up and transferred to the left hand, the jacks are all put in the right hand and scattered again. Proceed through twos, threes, fours, fives, and sixes.

Crack The Eggs

Scatter jacks with right hand. Toss ball with right hand and while ball bounces once, pick up one jack with right hand, "crack" (tap) it on the playing surface, and catch ball in right hand which is still holding the jack. Transfer the jack to the left hand and proceed as before until all jacks are picked up. Scatter again and proceed by twos, threes, etc., through sixes.

Upcast

Scatter jacks with right hand. Toss the ball with right, pick up one jack with right hand and catch the ball in the right hand after it has bounced once, same as in Baby Game. Toss the ball up again with the right hand and while it bounces transfer the jack to the left hand, and then catch the ball in the right hand. Continue until all jacks are in the left hand. Scatter again from the right hand and proceed by twos, then threes, etc., through sixes.

Downcast

This differs from Upcast in that the ball is started on the bounce by turning the palm of the hand toward the playing surface and then letting go of the ball.

Pigs In The Pen

Place left hand on the playing surface, finger tips and wrist touching the surface and forming the pen. Toss the ball upward and while it bounces again, pick up one jack with right hand and push it into the pen, then catch the ball in the right hand. Thumb and forefinger are lifted from the playing surface when jack is pushed in, but any jack or jacks left outside the thumb constitute a "miss". Scatter again with the right hand and proceed as before, putting jacks into the pen by twos, then by threes, etc., through sixes.

Pigs Over The Fence

Place left hand at right angles to the playing area, little finger resting on the playing surface. This forms the wall or fence. Scatter jacks, toss the ball upward with the right hand, and pick up one jack with the right hand. While ball bounces once, place the jack on the far side of the left hand (over the fence). When all six jacks are picked up, rescatter with the right hand and proceed by twos, threes, etc., through sixes.

Sweeps

Scatter jacks, toss ball, and while ball bounces once, place fingers on one jack and without lifting it from the playing surface, sweep it across the surface with the right hand until it is close to the body. Then pick it up and catch the ball with the same hand. Sweep all jacks singly; then rescatter and proceed sweeping by twos, then by threes, etc., through sixes.

Scrubs

Scatter jacks, toss ball, pick up one jack and scrub it across the playing surface with a backward and foreward movement. Keep jack in right hand and after ball has bounced once, catch the ball in the same hand. Transfer jack to the left hand and proceed until all six jacks have been "scrubbed." Rescatter and scrub by twos, then threes, etc., through sixes.

Double Bounce

This is played the same as the Baby Game, but ball must bounce twice before it is caught. Play through sixes.

Bounce, No Bounce

Scatter jacks with right hand. Toss ball upward, pick up one jack while ball bounces once and catch the ball in the right hand. With jack still in right hand, toss the ball upward with the right hand, transfer the jack to the left hand, and catch the ball in the right hand without allowing it to bounce. Continue until all jacks have been transferred to the left hand; then rescatter and proceed by twos, threes, etc.

JACKSTONES, WITHOUT A BALL

In the following games Jackstones probably bear a closer resemblance to traditional Knucklebone than those previously described. Like Jackstones, with Ball, this is a traditional American form and the whole play is much quicker and more difficult than with the ball.

ONES.——Scatter the jacks. Select one for tossing, choosing one that is interlocked, or so near to others that it could not easily be removed in the afterplay without stirring them, or else one that has rolled so far away that it would be hard to play.

Toss the jackstone and while it is in the air pick up one of the others and, holding it in the palm of the hand, catch the tossed one in the same hand. Place to one side the jack picked up, toss, pick up another, and so on until all five have been picked up and set aside.

TWOS. PIGS IN THE PEN. SWEEPS.——Similar to directions under Jackstones, With Ball, except that the jackstone is tossed rather than the ball.

Handball

ORIGIN:

Many centuries ago, the ancient Celts devised Handball, which was played in Ireland and England using four walls. It was introduced into the United States in the 1870's, where Four-Wall's popularity declined with the innovation of the one-wall game. Today there are over forty countries participating in International competition.

EQUIPMENT:

1 Ball made of hard rubber, 1 7/8 inches in diameter and weighing 2.3 ounces
hand gloves to protect hands in Four-Wall (optional)

OBJECTIVE:

The first player tries to keep the ball away from his opponent while hitting the ball against the wall.

RULES:

Handball is a game played by two or four persons on a one-wall or four-wall court. In theory, the court in the one-wall game is twenty feet by thirty-four feet. The short line, from behind which the ball is served, is marked off sixteen feet from, and parallel to, the wall, which is sixteen feet high.

In the city, however, the side of a building often serves as a wall, and the width of the street or playground determines the size of the court. (School yards are an all-time favorite.)

The server hits the ball, with either of his hands, against the wall before or after it has struck the floor once. He tries to hit the ball out of reach of his opponent, who tries to strike the ball against the wall. The serve changes hands when the server cannot return the ball.

SCORING:

Only when the non-server cannot return the ball against the wall is a point scored. The first player, or pair of players, to reach twenty-one points wins.

VARIATIONS:

Four-Wall Handball

The court is twenty-three feet by forty-six feet, and is surrounded by three walls each twenty-three feet high and a back wall twelve feet high. The ball can be played off any of the walls. All the rules and scoring of one-wall handball apply to this version.

DIAGRAM (HANDBALL):

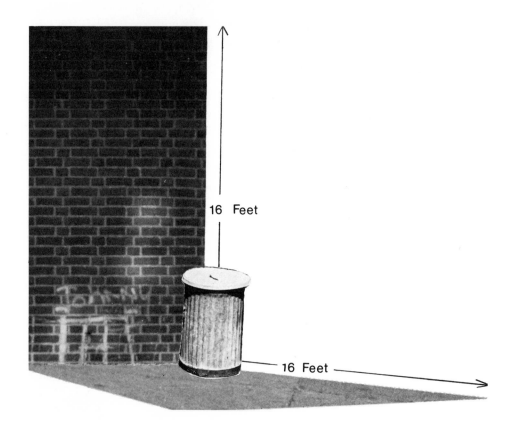

16 Feet

16 Feet

Chinese Handball (or Ace, King, Queen Jack,)

Four or five players stand in front of four or five corresponding adjacent spaces. Every ball must be hit onto the sidewalk or pavement before bouncing off the wall into a player's box. Once a ball is slapped into a player's box, he must return it after one bounce in his own box. If he fails to do so, he earns a strike and moves one box to the right. The line of players rotates each time a player misses the shot or bounce. Ten strikes against any one player eliminates him from the game.

A very confusing game requiring quick reflexes.

DIAGRAM:

Continuation, Telephone, and Aunt Mildred's Trunk

ORIGIN:

Continuation, a form of storytelling, is as old as the tradition of oral poetry. History was not written but recorded "on the minds" of men, each bard through the centuries updating the story. Homer would have enjoyed such activity as Continuation (or collective storytelling). Surely, he would have let as many people as wished to play, as long as he got the by-line.

Telephone closely parallels the tradition of telling stories -- with a technical twist. This modern derivative could not have been formalized without the invention of Bell's telephone in 1876, just a hundred years after the Revolution. (The telephone created one of its own, with over 290,000,000 telephones in the world today.)

Unlike Continuation and Telephone, Aunt Mildred's Trunk requires a good memory as well as imaginative storytelling. No one knows the origin of the game nor of Aunt Mildred.

OBJECT:

To reach the whole, which is usually greater than (and different from) the sum of its parts.

RULES:

Even when everyone's legs are tired, the mouth never seems to quit. This is the time for Telephone or Continuation, especially for those who love talking a blue streak, boring their friends, distorting the truth, embellishing facts, or having a chance to tell a secret they're sworn not to tell.

Continuation

Everyone gathers in a circle or straight line and counts off consecutively. Number one begins telling the story, using a topic of his choice, and continues non-stop for two minutes. One person must be timekeeper, who watches the clock and specifies "time's up" every two minutes. This signals the next person in line to take up the story where his predecessor left off. The new storyteller must follow the same line of thought when continuing the story.

However, as time moves on during his turn, he can vary the story by shifting logically from one topic to another. The game ends when everyone has gone once, everyone is talked out, or everyone has gone around the circle talking in circles. This is a very good introduction to group therapy.

Telephone

This game, a cross between Continuation and "I've Got a Secret," leaves greater room for surprise and invention. The final outcome in this traveling story is not revealed until the end of the game.

Those playing sit in a straight line, while the first person to put in a call prepares his brief (or lengthy) telephone conversation. He whispers the story into the ear of the person on his right. This second player, in turn, whispers it to the next person as he heard it. The story makes its way down the line by this mouthpiece-to-receiver communication until the final toll station is reached. The last player repeats aloud the message he received -- which, in theory, should resemble the original story. It never does. There is always at least one person who radically distorts, or removes the story along the way. Later in life, that person ends up working for an answering service. But even playing in good faith, Telephone reveals the juice of gossip.

Aunt Mildred's Trunk

Most people cannot recite more than nine numbers from memory though they often do better with words. One person starts with an opening phrase, such as: "I am going to visit Aunt Mildred and I'm going to pack a ... (toothbrush, or whatever else one decides to pack to take with him)."

The next person repeats the opening phrase and adds one more item to the ever-expanding suitcase. Each player in turn must recite the entire list of items packed, in the correct order, before making his own addition. Very often the items are totally unrelated to one another. It's very much like trying to memorize T. S. Eliot's "Sweeny Agonistes," except that Eliot would remember everything he listed and have a very specific reason for packing it in.

Some people try to be foxy and create acronyms, but even then there comes a time where there are too many letters to remember. If a player makes an error in reciting the list, he is out. The winner is the last person left packing.

DURAND J 5 r Emile Duclaux 15e... 734.90.87
DURAND Mme S
38 r Entrepreneurs 15e.......... 577.51.69
DURAND H reg rel feuil mob
44 r Enghien................ 770.46.30
DURAND Mlle I 4 r Erard 12e........ 345.16.34
DURAND march coul
6 r Ernest Cresson 14e......... 567.10.98
DURAND 17 r Ernest Cresson 14e.. 734.22.83
DURAND Mme C 1 r Ernest Lefèvre.. 797.40.41
DURAND J ing agron
14 r Ernest Psichari 7e......... 551.06.84
DURAND Mme Vve S 24 r Etex 18e.. 627.84.35
DURAND J 24 r Etex 18e........... 627.70.40
DURAND Mme M 2 r Etienne Marey 797.30.19
DURAND E 12bis r Etoile 17e......... 754.44.15
DURAND Mr Mme
11 r Eugène Flachat 17e......... 755.80.03
DURAND Mlle J 12 bd Exelmans 16e 527.30.99
..DURAND Janie 12 bd Exelmans 16e 527.40.63
DURAND M 74 bd Exelmans 16e....... 525.39.71
DURAND Mme J laver teint
11 r Faidherbe 11e.............. 357.71.38
DURAND R 8 r Fallempin 15e......... 306.49.98
DURAND M 3 r Fantin Latour 16e...... 288.83.53
DURAND J confect sport 7 r Fauvet 627.21.20
DURAND J 5 Pl Félix Eboué 12e....... 343.71.75
DURAND Y 119 av Félix Faure 15e... 533.36.23
DURAND J 3 r Fernand Pelloutier.. 228.07.17
DURAND A repr 8 r Fer à Moulin.... 535.55.95
DURAND P réalisat radio
3 r Fidélité 10e.................. 770.48.05
DURAND Mlles M et J
5 r Fidélité 10e.................. 770.35.12
DURAND J assist rech scientif
12 r Firmin Gillot 15e............ 250.58.55
DURAND G 10 r Flatters 5e.......... 336.06.73
DURAND E chauff mécan*
19 r Folie Regnault 11e............ 805.40.78
DURAND Mr Mme 52 r Fondary 15e.. 306.36.94
DURAND J 56 r Fondary 15e......... 306.20.33
DURAND MME J *Pommes de Terre* 59 r Fontaine au Roi.... 357.51.80
—même adresse...................... 357.51.81
—même adresse...................... 357.88.31
—même adresse...................... 357.51.82
DURAND J
44 r Fossés St Bernard 5e......... 633.91.12
..DURAND J 24 r Frémicourt 15e...... 567.58.72
DURAND Mme H 8 r Freycinet 16e..... 720.85.13
→ 727.92.41
DURAND G 6 sq Gabriel Fauré 17e.. 227.19.41
DURAND Mme D
1 villa Gagliardini 20e............ 366.91.14
DURAND C repr
4 villa Gagliardini................. 636.70.49
DURAND J-P 13 r Gandon 13e......... 589.38.76
DURAND H 39 r Garneron 18e......... 627.29.19
DURAND J-P 185 bd Gare 13e......... 588.64.38
DURAND 185 bd Gare 13e............. 707.32.78
DURAND M 4 r Gauthey 17e........... 228.06.38
DURAND C repr commerc
9bis r Gazan 14e.................. 588.63.28
DURAND M 27 r Gazan 14e............ 588.11.43
DURAND M 31 r Gazan 14e............ 588.35.63
DURAND Mme J 4 av Gén Balfourier. 288.97.25
DURAND M-L 7 r Gén Delestraint.... 288.43.03
DURAND N 3 r Gén Grossetti 16e.... 647.51.46
DURAND Mme J 110 av Gén Leclerc 532.63.92
DURAND Emmanuel
18 r Gén Malleterre 16e........... 647.46.64
DURAND H archit
117 av Gén Michel Bizot 12e..... 344.22.10
DURAND M 16 r Geoffroy l'Angevin. 272.97.77
DURAND A 8 r Geoffroy St Hilaire.... 707.70.39
DURAND M 49 r Geoffroy St Hilaire. 707.58.69
DURAND S 6 r Georges Lardennois 208.56.73
DURAND 31 r Georges Sand 16e..... 288.09.36
DURAND Mme A
13 r Georgette Agutte 18e 228.32.04
DURAND insp ppal adj chargé fonctions INP dir serv postaux
51 r Gérard 13e................... 588.86.03
DURAND Mr Mme 2 pass Gergovie.... 567.88.02
DURAND M 28 r Ginette Neveu 18e... 255.31.99
DURAND R radiotech
48 r Glacière 13e................. 587.13.29
DURAND M ing 16 bd Gouvion St Cyr 755.69.99
DURAND J-C programmeur analyste
74 r Grands Champs 20e........... 345.10.87
DURAND J-P 18 bd Grenelle 15e...... 577.06.25
..DURAND G 20 bd Grenelle 15e....... 577.07.65
DURAND G 125 bd Grenelle 15e 306.75.72
DURAND M teint 65 r Greneta 2e..... 236.54.15
DURAND J-C compt 10 r Gros 16e. 224.92.89
DURAND CH (ETS) caoutc
17 r Guersant 17e................. 754.47.78
DURAND Mme C 12 r Guichard 16e... 224.70.98
DURAND G 8 r Gustave Lebon 14e.... 250.60.00
DURAND H court en prod sol
9bis r Hainaut 19e................ 205.54.71
DURAND H 9bis r Hainaut 19e....... 205.12.74
DURAND P adm civ 18 r Hameau...... 250.08.56
DURAND M 3 r Harpe 5e............. 326.47.89
DURAND M avoc Cour appel
1 r Hauteville 10e................ 770.03.36
DURAND R 9 r Henri Poincaré 20e.... 636.54.38
DURAND R 8 r Herran 16e............ 704.38.70
DURAND M 12 r Hippolyte Lebas 9e 878.63.64
DURAND Mme R 4 av Hoche 8e........ 227.06.83
DURAND P compos
20 bd Hôpital 5e.................. 535.53.16
DURAND H 24 bd Invalides 7e........ 555.19.54
DURAND B prof math 44 bd Invalides. 783.36.54
DURAND M 76 av Italie 13e.......... 580.44.93
→ 707.44.93
DURAND J vins gr 11 r Jaucourt.... 343.72.51
DURAND M 7 r Jean Formigé 15e...... 532.44.64
DURAND M 94 av Jean Jaurès 19e.... 202.18.70
DURAND M 17 r Jean Leclaire 17e. 627.87.73
DURAND Mr Mme J-J
17 r Jean Mermoz 8e.............. 225.84.85
DURAND G 13 av Jean Moulin 14e.... 533.29.20
DURAND M 43bis av Jean Moulin.... 828.61.99

DURAND J 72 av Jean Moulin 14e.... 250.37.16
DURAND R dessinat
98 r Jean-Pierre Timbaud 11e 357.92.84
DURAND S prof math
13 r Jeanne Hachette 15e....... 250.23.84
DURAND Mlles H et M
82 qu Jemmapes 10e............ 203.33.31
DURAND R 12 r Jobbé Duval 15e ....
DURAND A 1 r Joseph Dijon 18e.....
DURAND P journaliste 3 r Jouffroy
DURAND P ing 44 r Jouffroy 17e...
DURAND G 17 r Jouvenet 16e.......
DURAND Rosine 22bis r Jouvenet....
DURAND R 1 sq Jules Chéret 20e.....
DURAND O 28 r Juliette Lamber....
DURAND J verrier 3 r La Boétie....
—même adresse......................
DURAND R 10 r Laborde 8e..........
..DURAND H
72 av La Bourdonnais 7e..........
DURAND C 30 r Labrouste 15e.......
DURAND M 62 r Labrouste 15e.......
DURAND Mr Mme A
28 r La Condamine 17e.............
DURAND G 18 r Lacretelle 15e......
DURAND Mlle M 32bis r Lacépède...
*DURAND J.C. chirurgien
43 r Lacépède 5e..................
DURAND C coiff 35 r Lacroix 17e....
DURAND P 13 r Lacuée 12e..........
DURAND R coiff p dam
17 r La Fontaine 16e...............
DURAND Mr Mme B
26 r La Fontaine 16e..............
DURAND P-F nég en vins
15 r Lagny 20e.....................
DURAND M brass 28 r Lagny 20e....
DURAND R 42 r Lagny 20e...........
..DURAND Ginette 46 r Lagny 20e....
DURAND J employé banque
15 r Lakanal 15e...................
DURAND D graphiste
33bis r Lamarck 18e...............
DURAND 98 r Lamarck 18e...........
DURAND R ing Ponts Chauss
52 av La Motte Picquet............
DURAND 52 av La Motte Picquet 7e.
DURAND L 14 r Langeac 15e..........
DURAND Mlle M-A 2 r Lantiez 17e....
DURAND R 5 r La Pérouse 16e.......
→
DURAND Mme 14 r Lapeyrère 18e.....
DURAND Mme J 14 r Lapeyrère 18e...
DURAND M 7 r Laplace 5e...........
DURAND R ing E.D.F.
37 r La Quintinie 15e..............
..DURAND G 44 r La Quintinie 15e....
DURAND P 31 r La Rochefoucauld 9e
DURAND R et Mme
76 bd Latour Maubourg 7e......... 705.48.94
DURAND G ajusteur outilleur
3 villa Laugier 17e............... 267.05.16
DURAND Mlle M 18 r Lauriston 16e 727.91.18
DURAND J ing 129 r Lauriston 16e. 553.30.24
DURAND Simonne 95 r Leblanc 15e 531.27.19
DURAND A secret 14 r Lebrun 13e.. 707.59.94
DURAND Mlle M 49 r Lecourbe 15e.. 566.01.91
DURAND J-P 127 r Lecourbe 15e.... 842.17.88
DURAND 51 bd Lefebvre 15e......... 250.08.37
DURAND M 59 bd Lefebvre 15e....... 532.46.00
DURAND M 85 bd Lefebvre 15e....... 842.55.29
DURAND J-P 105 bd Lefebvre 15e.... 842.52.69
DURAND A 119 bd Lefebvre 15e...... 828.50.72
DURAND J 59 r Legendre 17e........ 627.33.25
DURAND Mme F secrét
145 r Legendre 17e 627.33.51
DURAND R boucher 191 r Legendre 627.54.81
DURAND Mme Mr 17 r Lemercier..... 387.62.52
DURAND Mme M empl serv soc
53 r Léon Frot 11e................ 355.54.29
DURAND M secrét gén
12 r Léon Jouhaux 10e............. 607.93.42
DURAND Mme F vente de parf soins esthétiques 28 r Letort 18e...... 254.84.37
DURAND M 22 r Lévis 17e........... 924.28.07
DURAND J trip dét 25 r Lévis 17e.. 227.15.45
DURAND 71 r Lévis 17e............. 227.70.07
DURAND R 48 r Liancourt 14e....... 566.54.01
DURAND Mme J 10 r Linois 15e 578.07.26
DURAND J 14 r Loing 14e........... 589.15.72
DURAND B conseil ambass 5 r Lota 727.51.22
DURAND R 32 r Louis Braille 12e.... 345.32.71
DURAND 8 r Louis Ganne 20e........ 797.21.97
DURAND P méd
148 r Lourmel 15e................. 579.34.51
→ 842.34.51
DURAND M 164 r Lourmel 15e........ 577.96.45
DURAND Mme M 164 r Lourmel 15e.... 579.08.01
→ 532.08.01
DURAND H hte coiff 17 av Mac Mahon 754.42.07
DURAND M doct méd ch clin Fac
19 av Mac Mahon 17e.............. 380.28.39
DURAND et CIE édit musiq bur concert 4 pl Madeleine 8e........ 260.21.76
→ 073.62.19
—phonos disques même adresse. 260.20.01
→ 073.09.78
—même adresse..................... 073.41.62
→ 260.34.08
→ 073.45.74
DURAND Mme G 7 r Maillard 11e.... 805.29.86
DURAND D prof 43 av Maine 14e..... 633.08.94
DURAND J-P 190 av Maine 14e....... 273.05.97
DURAND J-J visit médic
193 av Maine 14e................. 306.79.20
DURAND A 194 av Maine 14e......... 734.08.79
DURAND A 1 sq Malherbe 16e........ 647.98.69
DURAND Mme R et Mr
200 bd Malesherbes 17e........... 924.62.31
DURAND G 7 r Malte 11e............ 805.15.22
DURAND Mme M 40 r Malte 11e...... 357.39.21
DURAND H et Mme 65 r Manin 19e... 205.28.56
DURAND R ing commerc
82 r Manin 19e................... 205.39.20

DURAND M 6 av Marcel Doret 16e.... 527.36.44
DURAND R crém 1 r Marcel Sembat 076.68.63
..DURAND A 33 r Marc Seguin 18e.. 206.93.45
DURAND G et M
10bis r Martin Bernard 13e..... 589.44.52
DURAND 7 r Marx Dormoy 18e........ 206.89.96
DURAND P 62 bd Masséna 13e........ 589.31.73
DURAND G crémier

51 r Moulin des Prés 13e.......... 589.30.57
DURAND M métr vérif
24 r Moulin Vert 14e............. 783.69.02
DURAND J-C et Mme repr
10 r Mounet Sully 20e............. 307.50.78
DURAND M archit
7 r Mousset Robert 12e............ 628.59.64
DURAND Mlle F 122 av Mozart 16e.. 224.92.71
DURAND Y 137 bd Murat 16e........ 647.09.02
DURAND Mme M-L 169 bd Murat..... 520.85.81
DURAND J-L assistant univ
20 r Nantes 19e.................. 203.47.27
DURAND M 41 bd Ney 18e............ 076.28.00
DURAND Mr Mme J-R
1 r Nicolas Charlet 15e.......... 273.36.21
DURAND H 67 r Nollet 17e.......... 627.87.18
DURAND P ing 74 r Nollet 17e...... 228.18.57
DURAND R 4 Cité Nollez 18e........ 606.51.74
DURAND libr
6 r Notre Dame de Lorette 9e..... 526.13.29
DURAND Mme M 140 r Oberkampf.. 357.97.22
DURAND R 54 r Olivier de Serres..... 533.49.12
DURAND J doct méd 203 r Ordener 228.04.00
DURAND R nettoy gén 34 bd Ornano 076.36.45
DURAND J-C entrepr nettoy
67 r Orteaux 20e.................. 797.78.03
DURAND A doct méd
6 r Ouessant 15e.................. 567.04.04
DURAND G-A biologiste
10 r Ouessant 15e................. 273.39.55
DURAND J entrepr maçonn
122 r Ouest 14e.................. 532.65.85
DURAND A fonctionnaire 123 r Ouest 842.50.88
DURAND Mme F 48 av Parmentier.... 700.05.64
DURAND M-T insp trésor
156 av Parmentier 10e............ 202.40.02
DURAND L coiff 15 r Parrot 12e..... 307.90.02
DURAND Mme Y 6 r Pâtures 16e..... 525.39.24
DURAND H sénateur
33 r Paul Barruel 15e............ 250.63.32
DURAND M-J 55 r Paul Barruel 15e 533.13.14
DURAND G 9 r Paul Bodin 17e....... 229.45.00
DURAND C 12 r Paul Bodin 17e 627.51.09
DURAND R insp central P.T.T.
23 r Paul Fort 14e................ 589.91.61
DURAND H 5 r Péguy 6e 548.21.94
DURAND Mme G et Mr secrét
20 r Perdonnet 10e................ 206.45.88
DURAND P archit 156 bd Péreire 754.85.10
DURAND J 177 bd Péreire 17e....... 924.57.76
DURAND B 182bis bd Péreire 17e.... 754.01.16
DURAND Mr Mme D
197 bd Péreire 17e............... 754.81.30
DURAND 206 bd Péreire 17e......... 380.23.27
DURAND G 1 pl Péreire 17e.......... 622.33.96
DURAND M 85 r Petit 19e........... 203.53.46
DURAND Mlle M 19 r Petits Champs 742.20.69
DURAND G 36 r Petits Hotels 10e.... 824.67.94
DURAND J-M 53 r Peupliers 13e..... 588.20.56
DURAND G 85 bd Picpus 12e......... 345.13.92
DURAND P 118 r Picpus 12e......... 345.26.16
DURAND C 124 r Picpus 12e......... 307.52.92
DURAND P repr 24 r Pigalle 9e..... 744.24.46
—même adresse..................... 744.39.59
DURAND P-J repr 24 r Pigalle 9e.... 874.12.18
DURAND Mme Vve P 20 r Plaisance. 567.60.42

DURAND E 12 villa Poirier 15e........ 306.58.30
DURAND L grav imprim
54 r Faub Poissonnière 10e...... 770.81.06
DURAND L ing
126 r Faub Poissonnière 10e... 878.43.48
DURAND E
134 r Faub Poissonnière 10e... 526.94.96
DURAND C conseil jurid
b Poissonnière 9e..... 874.92.44
r Pompe 16e.......... 704.01.10
av Porte de Choisy... 588.12.43
rt
Porte Montmartre 18e. 076.32.23
te de Vincennes 12e.. 808.
é 75 r Pouchet 17e... 627.
E 5 r Poulet 18e...... 076.63.
r Présentation 11e..... 355.95.
gén 67 r Prony 17e... 924.16.7
r Pyrénées 20e........ 636.19.44
me L 383 r Pyrénées 797.96.01
ères Peignot 15e....... 577.19.17
Rachel 18e............ 387.68.33
r Rambouillet 12e...... 345.53.1
diste 48 r Ramey 18e 076.20.68
r conseil
pail 6e.................. 222.36.87
R 2 r Raynouard 16e. 647.89.81
t nez gorge oreil
mur 2e.................. 236.74.94
me 10 r Regard 6e...... 544.15.65
émy de Gourmont 19e. 202.81.57
B
Coty 14e............... 331.90.05
mmerc
6e..................... 548.06.13
r Rennes 6e............ 222.58.69
p ppal impôts
ublique 10e............ 700.23.51
Reuilly 12e........... 628.15.64
mob 23 bd Reuilly..... 344.11.51
r Reuilly 12e.......... 628.63.09
is r Réunion 20e...... 366.05.08
r Ribéra 16e........... 224.72.58
r Riquet 19e........... 607.10.46
e D 47 r Rivoli 1er.... 236.54.65
r Rivoli 1er............ 260.64.31
→ 073.22.24
lla Robert Lindet 532.17.61
Roche ... 11e........... 355.69.95
me L
hechouart 18e........... 255.65.41
Rochechouart 9e........ 878.19.
me M 23 r Rocroy 9e. 280.22.06
r Romainville 19e...... 208.96.82
conseil 103 r Rome..... 924.04.97
dét 112 r Roquette 11e.. .94.9
r Rosenwald 15e......... 532.36.76
DURAND R 9 r Rosière 15e......... 579.30.31
→ 250.30.31
DURAND P 40 r Rouelle 15e......... 577.41.03
DURAND P pharm 46 r Rouelle 15e 577.15.11
DURAND P 5 sq Roule 8e........... 924.52.58
DURAND A 8 r Rouvet 19e........... 607.68.85
DURAND P vend 57 r Ruisseau 18e 252.16.75
DURAND Denise
24 r St Charles 15e.............. 577.24.17
DURAND J étiqu p étal
22 bd St Denis 10e............... 770.62.20
DURAND M-L 89 r Faub St Denis..... 523.11.10
DURAND A repr 105 r Faub St Denis 824.85.97
DURAND P doct méd
9 r St Didier 16e................ 553.05.1
DURAND M
8 r Saint Julien le Pauvre 5e . 326.61.7
DURAND A ing 69 r St Fargeau 20e.. 636.50.28
DURAND J-C chirurgien
80 bd Saint Germain 5e.......... 033.54.56
DURAND J-M 152 bd St Germain 6e 033.01.62
DURAND Mme R 7 r St Hippolyte.... 587.14.91
DURAND R charc
310 r St Honoré 1er.............. 260.42.99
→ 073.37.45
DURAND O 12bis r Ste Isaure 18e.. 076.26.31
DURAND boucher 239 r St Jacques 633.15.15
DURAND Y 320 r St Jacques 5e...... 033.64.39
DURAND J-J
27 r St Louis en L'isle 6e........ 633.30.30
DURAND J 22 av St Mandé 12e 628.80.12
DURAND P insp ppal R.A.T.P.
102bis av St Mandé 12e.......... 307.78.46
DURAND Mr et Mme
10 bd St Marcel 5e............... 336.25.26
DURAND R 76 bd St Marcel 5e....... 535.92.00
DURAND M 134 Faub St Martin 10e. 206.94.65
DURAND crem dét
147 r St Martin 3e............... 278.07.59
→ 887.07.59
DURAND G compt 143 bd St Michel. 633.04.00
DURAND J 139 av St Ouen 17e...... 228.37.49
DURAND P 30 r St Paul 4e........... 277.80.76
DURAND H 75 r Sts Pères 6e....... 548.54.51
DURAND Mme R 75 r Sts Pères 6e.... 222.86.93
DURAND L moniteur 8 pl St Sulpice 633.86.62
DURAND C artis 30 r Saussure 17e. 924.05.57
DURAND J 11 r Sédillot 7e.......... 551.53.46
DURAND E impr 18 r Séguier 6e..... 326.84.56
DURAND J 5 r Serret 15e............ 828.70.76
DURAND R-A 14 bd Sérurier 19e .. 205.50.21
DURAND L boucher 18 r Siam 16e.... 504.54.67
DURAND G 41 av Simon Bolivar 19e. 202.60.46
DURAND Mme Mr boulang pâtiss
64 av Simon Bolivar 19e......... 208.34.34
DURAND L boucher 20 r Singer..... 527.39.96
DURAND J 29bis r Solidarité 19e.... 205.66.74
DURAND P 7 r Sophie Germain 14e. 707.80.17
DURAND P cadre adm 51 bd Soult... 628.51.53
DURAND R ing 53 bd Soult 12e....... 628.44.85
DURAND S ing 68 bd Soult 12e....... 307.02.55
DURAND grav lapid 14 pass Soupirs 636.85.93
DURAND Mme L 28 r Spontini 16e.... 704.52.42
DURAND R 5 av Stéphen Pichon 13e. 331.63.69
DURAND A dir régional
79 bd Suchet 16e................. 288.38.64
DURAND J 132 bd Suchet 16e....... 288.09.30

LANGUAGE

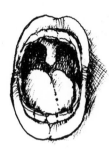

"There are plenty of hard words there. 'Brillig' means four o'clock in the afternoon—the time when you begin broiling things for dinner."
"That'll do very well," said Alice: "and 'slithy'?"
"Well, 'slithy' means 'lithe and slimy.' 'Lithe' is the same as 'active.' You see it's like a portmanteau—there are two meanings packed up into one word."

Humpty Dumpty's analysis of Jabberwocky
"Through the Looking Glass"
Lewis Carroll

The very first word, oral or written, is buried deep in time in the jungles, mountains, and deserts of the pre-historic world. Though neither Java nor Neanderthal man spoke, Cro-Magnon man developed a vocal tract enabling him to utter distinctive syllables. Written language, a later invention, is evidenced from Sumerian clay tablets that were chiseled with pictorial symbols and dating back to about 3500 B.C.

No one knows (or has yet discovered) the origin of the first children's language. Though language, in theory, was devised to allow communication, and thus further understanding between people, the languages of the young are devised backward -- intentionally to build barriers, to shut out unsympathetic listeners, to widen the generation gap, and to bind together only the small segment of the population that inhabits the children's world.

But we do have to wonder if perhaps such is justified reaction to adult language exclusions and gossip. For example, an American child present among older relatives suddenly hears, *der kinde,"* and the conversation may switch into German, Yiddish, or a tongue unfamiliar to the younger generation. Alienated youth can only retalliate with such gymnastic linguistics as Pig Latin or Gibberish. (Jabberwocky made that clear.)

Most kids are fascinated with language and sound, and they often develop new variations before they can barely and properly speak their national tongue. Much is learned by ear. Many under-fives still think that LMNOP is one word, and teenagers who sing "Frere Jacques" in a flash (though sounds become "mushed up" toward the third verse), may not have the faintest idea what the words mean. Repetition is the learning process here, and even what young people talk about is learned by ear and taken unquestioned, often, as fact.

Regardless, too, of proficiency in their own language, youngsters start at an early age to develop the most complex and difficult ways to communicate, to the total confusion of the world. The oldest surviving tongue, child or adult, is Chinese, and most adults agree that most children's tongues (rarely at rest, moving lightning fast, and mostly inarticulately) might as well be Chinese.

The two key elements needed to devise a lasting children's language are repetition and the restructured garble of syllabic tongue twisters that distort the mother tongue. When a sentence has been converted so that no one uninitiated understands the message, a terrific language has been born.

Dialectic differences carry over into the special languages of kids. If several sections of the country, all speaking Pig Latin, got together at the same place at the same time, it would be a remake of the linguistics convention held some many years back at the Tower of Babel.

In addition to regional accents, different age groups have different needs, and their communication reflects those needs -- whether it be Morse Code for the young; compulsive, secret language for the mistrusting adolescent; or sign language for the person who never wants to be misquoted.

INTERNATIONAL MORSE CODE:

A .-	N -.	Z ---.
B —...	O ----	1 .----
C -.-.	P .--.	2 ..---
D -..	Q --.-	3 ...--
E .	R .-.	4 ....-
F ..-.	S ...	5 .....
G --.	T -	6 -....
H	U ..-	7 --...
I ..	V ...-	8 ---..
J .---	W .--	9 ----.
K -.-	X -..-	0 -----
L .-.-	Y -.--	Comma .-.-.-
M --		period ......

SIGN LANGUAGE:

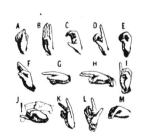

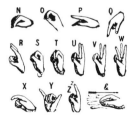

SECRET LANGUAGES:

(Technical and actual spoken practice occasionally differ.)

Pig Latin (Romantic)

The first letter or phonetic sound of each syllable is tacked onto the end of the remaining word with an *ay*. Leave one syllable words starting with a vowel the same and add yay (pronounced yeah!) to it.

Calvin Coolidge
Al-cay-in-vay   Oo-cay-idge-lay

The Lord is my shepherd, I shall not want
He-tay ord-lay is-yay y-may epherd-shay, I-yay al-shay ot-nay ant-way.

Ob

After every consonant an *ob* is added. Y is the only exception and remains unaltered.

Harry F. Truman
Hob-a-rob-roby Fob. Tob-rob-u-mob-a-nob

King Tut

All the vowels stay the same. A *u* is added to every consonant, and the *u* is enclosed by the original consonant, i.e., *t* equals tut. All double consonants are expressed as square, i.e., nn equals nun-square (the slight mathematical touch lends legitimacy). Every y is converted into yuk. *All separate vowels are pronounced long, except u's which are short.*

She sells sea shells by the sea shore
Sus-huh-e sus-e-lul-square-sus sus-ea sus-huh-e-lul-square-sus bub-yuk tut-huh-e sus-e-a sus-huh-o-rur-e

Teddy Roosevelt
Tut-e-dud-square-yuk Rur-o-square-sus-e-vuv-e-lul-tut

Gibberish

An *itha* is added to the initial consonant of the syllable and all the vowels are preceded with a g, i.e., book equals bitha-gook; before equals bitha-gee fitha-gore.

George Washington
Githa-george Witha-gash-itha-ging-titha-gon

How much wood could a woodchuck chuck, if a woodchuck could chuck wood?
Hitha-gow mitha-guch witha-good citha-gould itha-ga witha-good chita-guck chita-guck, itha-gif itha-ga, witha-good chitha-guck citha-gould chitha-guck witha-good?

Op

Op is added to the first consonant of each syllable and the remaining portion of the syllable is preceded with an f. All syllables that start with a vowel get the preceding f.

Herbert Hoover
Hop-fer-bop-fert Hop-foo-vop-fer

If Peter Piper picked a peck of pickled peppers,
Where's the peck of pickled peppers Peter Piper picked?
Fif Pop-fet-top-fer Pop-fip-pop-fer pop-ficked fa pop-feck fof pop-fick-lop-fed pop-fep-pop-fers
Whop-fere's thop-fe pop-feck fof pop-fick-lop-fed pop-fet-pop-fers
Pop-fet-top-fer Pop-fip-pop-fer pop-ficked?

The 2nd Quarter

FASHIONS

Marbles
London Bridge
Leap Frog
Jump Rope
Touch-Tag Football
Hopscotch
Stare, Blinking, Silence
Stretch
King of the Mountain

THE NEW KID

FASHIONS

The earliest clothing showing style-sense was the mini-skirt, or skin brief, worn by cave-children. As thousands of years evolved, man began adding layer upon layer of garments, girdles, hoops, and corsets to his attire. People spent half their lives dressing (small wonder so many died at early ages).

By the middle of the 20th century, the cumbersome trend began to reverse itself, the gap between Neanderthal and 20th century becoming less and less. Each successive period, though, was filled with a wide variety of styles, adult fashions and children's alike. In the Middle Ages, children wore clothes influenced by religious trends; the Renaissance through the 19th century saw them emulating their parents--from the festooned, puffy, proper, stiff, stark, tight protective garb to the fitted, comfortable and casual dress of today.

Clothes were also an indicator of wealth, class, and nationality. As more and more European families moved to the New World, fashions quickly changed into radically new styles reflecting economic status or religion, rather than the dress of any particular national heritage.

The 20th century especially brought about the age of the hand-me-down, where one kid was likely to wear the pants or sweater of an older brother or sister, cousin, or even parent -- a pair of new play pants could conceivably be thirty years old and worn by six pairs of legs before hitting the dust. (Novel to think of a child by the age of ten having been in four other people's pants.)

Most children, throughout the centuries, seem to cherish their play clothes -- far more than school outfits and formal wear. The rich exception, however, is when they play at Dress Up, wild in fashion and invention.

I played dress up, from morning to night; usually in my older, and only, sister Jerry's best clothes, when she was away at school. I played store, in our neighbor's backyard. Mud pies were sold to the various mothers in the neighborhood. I played shows, and always cast myself in the most violent parts. I was always the villain. As for games, I never played them.

—Mary Martin

Mary Martin

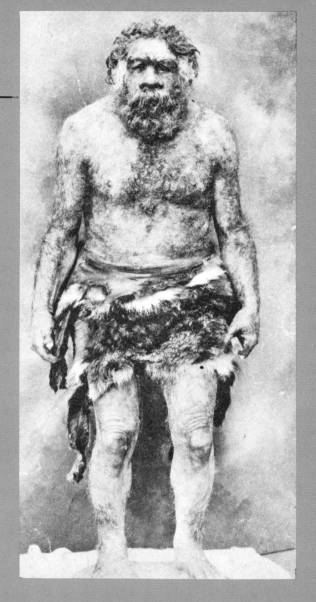

Cave Period—Cave children emulated the adults'
fashionable dress of mini-skins designed by leopards,
antelope, and others whose hides were ''the'' dress of
the day.

1400's Mini-caftans were
the maximum for play
when 'au naturel' was
out (which wasn't too
often).

Ieux de Crecerelle, Moulinet, & autres.

The 1500's--The Monk-Look variations on priestly robes were adorned with sashes, capes, and wide belts, in keeping with the trends of the times.

Kinder-Spiel / oder Spiegel dieser Zeiten.

1600--Shakespeare-in-the-Park look. Children were less supressed in the time of Elizabeth, and children were unlikely to do handstands or cartwheels in a monk's robe. Thus, two-piece suits worn with tights were more comfortable and less embarrassing for their up-side-down play.

1700's--The Lilliputian line of clothing, at its height of parental imitation. All the kids were miniature mommies and daddys, short, overstuffed bundles of clothing running around. These outfits were restrictive, very stuffy, and not conducive to raucus play.

Culver

Although in the 1800's kids were slowly allowed to be kids once again, the dress codes still remained stiff. The age of girdles and straight-jackets, however, had come to a close. Tied around britches, long-socked undergarments, turnback hats, visor caps, plaid jackets made of worsted wool, and tuck jackets with a welted seam front and back, made up the general play outfit.

Street Games 87

Above: The 1920's--Pre-depression disarray. Less formal, unmatched clothing, but still wearing hard leather shoes (lace and button tops), shirts with sleeves rolled up (no T-shirt yet), and suspenders.

Culver

Left: The 1910's—Jackie Coogan, era caps, cut-off overalls (cotton), long socks, rib knitted sweaters over a light sweater or longjohns (buttoned all the way down) gave playclothes the fashion of that day.

Culver

The 1930's--Sailor-boy collars, knickers smock dresses, short socks, shoes instead of boots, shorts and patterned socks were all in.

Culver

Street Games   89

Culver

Above: The 1940's—The smart look. Sweat pants, pea-jackets, T-shirts, moccasins, and oxfords were all part of the fall and spring lines. Children have always loved wearing hats belonging to uniforms, but it was especially popular during W.W.II.

Below: 1950's. Joe Namath even then was the height of fashion in his plaid shirt and patterned suspenders. Also popular were sailor caps, baggy pants, and chinos. Everyone can remember the girls in their regulation felt mid-calf skirts, cinch-elastic belts, tucked-in sweaters, high bobby socks, and saddle or suede shoes.

Culver

Above left and right: Dressing up, always in season, always in fashion.

Above: The 1960's—Chinos were replaced by corduroy pants with cuffs, many with bib tops. Outdoor jackets required emblems on sleeves, front and/or back. Footwear tended toward crepe soles and high sneakers. As the decade ended, "cords" lost favor to denim jeans that flared from the knee and rarely had cuffs. Belts became wider and hush puppies or low slung sailing sneakers gained popularity. As for the 1970's, the photographs in this book speak for themselves.

Marbles

The little b Play.

T A W.

KNUCKLE down to your *Taw*,
Aim well, fhoot away ;
Keep out of the *Ring*,
And you'll foon learn to play.

M O R A L.

Time rolls like a *Marble*,
And awes ev'ry State ;
Then hufband each Moment,
Before 'tis too late.

HOOP

*From The Little Pretty
Pocketbook published in 1744
by An Act of Parliament.*

ORIGIN:

Marbles were probably played by cavemen with small pebbles. There are references to Roman children playing a form of the game in which nuts were rolled down an incline in an effort to hit the nuts resting on the ground. The game seems more to resemble the principles of Bowling than Marbles. The game was also well known in Egypt well before Anno Domini.

The children of the American colonists played Marbles, and the game has not only survived but flourished in every state of the Union. Samuel Dyke manufactured the first marble, which was made of clay, in the United States in 1884. Small glass balls are the most recent addition to the long history of marbles.

Generally, marble manufacturers buy clean scrap glass—pop bottles, mustard jars, pickle jars, etc.—in order to make quality marbles which won't crack easily in play.

After the glass is collected (scrap glass or silica sand), soda ash is added as a fluxing agent. Ash is to glass-making what cement is to concrete mixing. Finally, other assorted ingredients are added for color, texture, etc. All of it is dumped into a large furnace which rages at 2300 degrees Fahrenheit for 15-18 hours, rendering a molten glass with the consistency of molasses. At last the liquid is poured into molds to form glass balls. Believe it or not, the most expensive glass is red glass and the least expensive is crystal, which is not used in the manufacture of marbles.

Beside providing hours of gamesmanship, marbles are now being used to roll crypts easily into place in mausoleums.

Every day, there are over three-million marbles manufactured in West Virginia alone. Germany and Japan have closed their glass manufacturing plants because of a shortage of natural resources. There are only six plants left in the world—four in the United States and two in Mexico—which supply the world market. The game is as popular as ever, though some countries have lost their marbles.

RULES:

There is such a wide range of opinion on the types, names, and rules of any one game that one universal set of rules would please no more than two or three players. There are hundreds of conflicts between history, old-timers, youngsters, experts, and casual players that make generalizing impossible. Recognizing this problem, the rules from the Veterans of Foreign Wars Tournament have been put forth as samples. Localities will have to fight it out among themselves.

RING. (See diagram below.) On a smooth, level area of hard clay, or other suitable substance, inscribe a ring ten feet in diameter, inside measurement. The outline of the ring should be approximately one-half inch wide and one-half inch deep.

With the center of the ring as a point of intersection, mark or paint two lines at right angles to each other to form a cross on which to place the playing marbles. Place one marble at the center and three each on the four branches of the cross, each marble three inches away from the next one.

Establish a lag line by drawing a straight line tangent to the ring and touching it at one point. Directly across the ring and parallel to the lag line, draw another straight line tangent to the ring to serve as the pitch line.

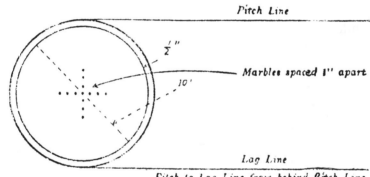

Pitch to Lag Line from behind Pitch Line

MARBLES. The marbles must be round, made of glass, and of uniform size measuring not more than five-eighths of an inch in diameter.

The shooters may be made of any substance except metal, must be round and not less than one-half inch nor more than three-fourths inch in diameter by exact measurement.

PLAYERS. Only two players may play in a game in a championship match.

THE LAG. Before the game the players lag to determine the order of shooting. To lag, they stand toeing the pitch line or knuckling down upon it, and toss or shoot their shooters to the lag line across the ring. The player whose shooter comes nearest the lag line, on either side, wins the lag and the privilege of shooting first. The same shooter that is used in the lag must be used in the game following the lag. Boys lag together on the official's count. (1-2-lag.)

If the loser of the first game did not have a shot, he shall shoot first in the second game. The lag will be used again in the third game.

PLAYING RULES. Each player in turn knuckles down just outside the ring line, at any point he chooses, and shoots into the ring to knock one or more marbles out of the ring. A player must knuckle down on all shots so that at least one knuckle is in contact with the ground, and he must maintain this position until the shooter has left his hand.

Marbles knocked out of the ring are credited to the player knocking them out and the player continues to shoot from the spot where his shooter comes to rest. If a shooter goes outside of the ring, after shooting a marble out, the player recovers it and continues by shooting from the ring line, taking "roundsters" if desired, that is, shooting from any point around the ring.

After a miss, a player picks up his shooter and holds it until his next turn and then takes roundsters and shoots from any point of the ring line.

Whenever a marble or shooter comes to rest in the groove marking the ring, it is considered out of the ring.

If a shooter slips from a player's hand and the player calls "slips," the referee may order "no play" and permit the player to shoot again, provided the shooter does not travel more than ten inches and the referee is convinced it was an actual slip.

Marbles knocked out of the ring are to be picked up by the ring official.

SCORING. The player first obtaining seven marbles is the winner of the game, providing that on obtaining the seventh marble the shooter also goes out of the ring. If the shooter remains in the ring on this shot, the marble or marbles knocked out on this shot are respotted on the cross line, the shooter picked up, and the shot counted as a miss. All marbles knocked out prior to the last shot are kept by the shooter.

FOULS AND PENALTIES. It is a foul if a player—

1.—Raises his hand before the shooter has left his hand. Penalty: the player loses his shot.

2.—Moves his hand forward before the shooter has left his hand. Penalty: the player loses his shot.

3.—Smooths or otherwise rearranges the ground or removes any obstacles. He may request the referee to clear obstructions. Penalty: the player loses his shot.

4.—Changes shooter during the course of any game, unless the shooter becomes broken, cracked or extremely chipped. Penalty: disqualification.

5.—Communicates in any way with his coach during the course of the game. Penalty: forfeiture of all marbles he has knocked out of the ring, said marbles being respotted on the cross.

6.—Walks through the ring. Penalty: forfeiture of one marble, which is respotted.

7.—If not in prescribed uniform the match will be forfeited.

Black beauties

Mibs

Lop-sided clay

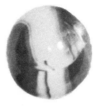

Cats eyes

Rainbow reeler

Swirled glass

Blood rubies

Crockies--Clay marbles

Clearys

Moon naggies

"The cheat at marbles." - 1850

95

VARIATIONS:

This informal game has been recognized by no one. First, it is necessary to convert a cigar box into a machine which collects marbles. Five arches are cut into the box, each equi-distant from the other along the upper edge. The first arch should be no wider than the width of a marble, and each successive hole increases in width and size. The smallest hole is labeled number 5 and the numbers, inversely proportional to size, decrease as the hole enlarges (see diagram).

The box is turned upside-down and placed against the curb so that the arches face into the street. The player shoots his marbles from a line about ten feet from the box. The object is to hit the cigar box without getting the marble in one of the holes. Each numbered hole represents the number of marbles the shooter must forfeit to his opponents. The box is fairly designed considering other games. A really good player can build his collection to gigantic proportion at the end of a good day at the box.

DIAGRAM:

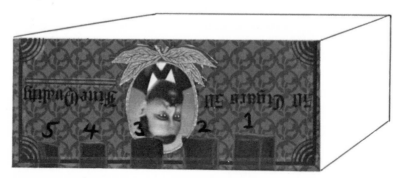

London Bridge

l3th Century wood-engraving

ORIGIN:

London Bridge is comprised of a catching game (the bridge) and a Tug of War, each with its own unique history. Being caught by the Bridge simply separated the players into two distinct and incompatible groups--devils and angels. In keeping with the theology of the Middle Ages, every man's soul separated from the body and journeyed either to the sacred, celestial sphere or the profane, infernal underworld. Those who were caught were destined to hell, and the other players took their heavenly bodies and formed one side of a human chain that would battle in the symbolic struggle between good and evil in the final Tug of War. (Tug of War was most likely added during the Middle Ages to enhance the significance of the "battle.")

Even before the Middle Ages emphasized the conflict between good and evil the building of a bridge was greeted with great suspicion. The people believed the land, or earth, was occupied by evil spirits. All the devilish creatures living in the soil supposedly liked their solitude. A bridge not only invaded this privacy, but connected one area with another that had previously been separate. The invasion aroused the anger of the devils, and a bridge built by day could expect trouble by nightfall. To appease the disturbed spirits, a child was sacrificed. (On a human level, the "evil spirits" may have represented man's own desire for solitude, his selfishness, and fear of new and different people.) Since there is no way to distinguish between young devils or angels today, the religious interpretation of the Tug of War and London Bridge has been dropped.

OBJECT:

To divide a group of players into two teams through a cheerful song and then to test the strength of the two teams by a tug of war.

RULES:

Two players face each other, clasping one another's hands high in front of themselves to form a bridge. The other players walk (or run) under the bridge in a procession. The players forming the bridge begin the chant and sing the verses alternately with the players passing under it. In most parts of the country, the bridge lowers its gates on the words, "My fair lady," capturing the person traveling through at that moment. The captured victim stands to one side of the bridge as the song continues while more players are trapped one-by-one. The victims alternately go to one side of the bridge or the other. Once everyone has been caught, each team member grasps the waist in front of him, forming a human rope or chain, and the Tug of War begins. Whichever side pulls the other over a designated line, wins.

London Bridge before 1561.

𝕿𝖍𝖊 𝕮𝖍𝖆𝖓𝖙 *(Sung as players go under bridge)*

London Bridge is falling down, falling down, falling down
London Bridge is falling down,
My fair lady.

Build it up with iron bars,
Iron bars, iron bars,
Build it up with iron bars,
My fair lady.
     etc.

"London Bridge" (officially Tower Bridge)

Leapfrog

"If I could win a lady at leapfrog"
Henry the Fifth V. ii. 140.

ORIGIN:

There are ancient references to Leapfrog in literature and art, but it was not until the Middle Ages that the game hit Europe in a big way. In paintings, Breughel to Hayman, as well as in the streets, Leapfrog made many frequent and diversified appearances. Today there are more than a dozen variations. The spell is cast: but unlike the fairy tale, there are more frogs and fewer princes today.

OBJECTIVE:

Regardless of the particular variation, one common element runs through all the games. One or more runners vaults over the back or backs of another player (or more).

RULES:

In its unaltered form, one player is the "back" and the other is the "jumper." The back bends over and holds his ankles, adjusting himself into a high- or low-back position by moving his hands up or down. The jumper is allowed to take a running start from the pre-designated starting line before vaulting over the back. Both the jumper's hands should be open and flatly placed on the back when the vault is made. For it to be considered a successful leap, the jumper should land on his two feet without falling over.

After the vault, either the two players reverse jobs, or the jumper, once securely landed on the ground, bends over and becomes the back, while the back stands upright, transforming himself into a frog (without even a kiss).

Engraving by Francis Hayman-1854.

The little m Play.

LEAP-FROG.

THIS ſtoops down his Head,
    Whilſt that ſprings up high;
But then you will find,
    He'll ſtoop by and by.

MORAL.

Juſt ſo 'tis at Court;
    To-day you're in Place;
To-morrow, perhaps,
    You're quite in Diſgrace.

BIRDS-

From The Little Pretty Pocketbook published in 1744 by an Act of Parliament.

VARIATIONS:

Over and Down and Up

This is the same as the simple form of Leapfrog, when there are more than two players. The group lines up behind the starting line, with the exception of one member who is the first back. After the first jumper goes and lands, he must take three steps forward before converting himself into a back. This leaves space for the following jumper.

Each succeeding jumper turns into a back upon landing until everyone has gone from a standing position by the starting line. In addition, each successive player must jump the increasing line of backs. Once the last leaper on line has leaped (by his turn that would mean at least six backs), the first back stands up and leaps over all the backs before him. When he comes to the end of the line, he becomes the last back on a never-ending line of jumping frogs.

The game can be made more difficult if each back moves closer together than the prescribed three feet, limiting the jumper's room to gain momentum. The confusion really sets in, though, after each back gets up to jump, once he's been leaped over by the preceding back-turned-jumper. The speed of the game accelerates so rapidly that by the time each one finishes a leap and bends down into a back, the next player is right on the "back" of his tail, vaulting over him. Without a rest, it's up again, and onto the next leap in the cycle. The leaping chain goes on until someone in the group reaches the Canadian or Mexican border.

Leader and Footer

The first person on the line is the leader and the last, the footer. The footer sets a specific approach pattern to follow before taking off over the first back. Three hops, a jump, a skip or two; three claps and two hops; a sneeze, a whistle, a wink and one plie are the types of stunts the footer requests before each player takes his leap.

However ridiculous, the leader at the head of the line must follow the footer's orders. The philosophy is strange and violates most conventional teachings. After all, the head rarely relies on what the foot is telling it.

Everyone must complete the folly, including the footer. The first person to err or fail the task becomes the back in the next game. After having had their turns leaping over the back, the footer redesigns the running pattern until he is unable to meet his own challenge. The shorter the distance between the starting line and the back, the less complicated the tasks will be. If the footer is challenged by another player, he must perform his own task first. If he's double-jointed, the group is in trouble.

Leapfrog Race

The players line up single-file in two separate lines. The first player runs to the starting line and bends over into a back. The next team member jumps over the first back and becomes the second back, upon which the third runner will leap -- and so on. Each player makes a series of leaps, one leap more than the player before him (who is by then a back). Both teams leap on their own players during this tumultuous race.

After everyone has had his turn, the first player stands up and leaps over his teammates' backs. At the end of his multiple vault, he stands up. Each player does this until every player has jumped over the back of every other player. The first team with one back left wins.

To add variety to the race, the pattern of leaping can be slightly altered. In Up and Down, each player crawls under a set of legs and vaults over a back, alternating the routine with each player.

Spanish Fly (or Leap-Leap)

As in Leader and Footer, the first person vaulting a back leaps in a unique fashion. One hand touching the back's head, clapping on the way over, knuckling (leaping over, placing the fists on a back as opposed to the prescribed open hand), landing on one foot, are among some of the imaginative choices open to a leader. All the followers must duplicate the feat. Whoever misses becomes the back.

Hatsies

The leader, as he jumps, places his hat on the back. The trick is to clear the back without touching or knocking off the hat. Each player, in turn, adds his hat to the pile, each time increasing the height required to clear the back.

Anyone who kicks over the hats is the new back. If the last player clears all the hats, the game reverses itself, and each player successively removes his hat without disturbing the others. When all the hats are back on their owners' heads, the game is over.

Saddle the Nag

A pony is formed as in Johnny on the Pony (see page 168). The first member of the opposing team leaps onto the "nag" and creeps his way forward while the nag tries to bronco-bust him off (without actually standing up). By comparison, this makes riding bareback a massage. If the rider makes his way to the pillow, he "crowns" him. (Crown is not the usual administering of a blow to the head, but another name for tagging the pillow -- though the former definition frequently applies.) Most runners, however bruised and battered, find themselves on the ground before they even come close to the pillow.

Every member of the running team gets a chance to reach the summit, or pillow, before the side changes positions. After five rounds, the team delivering the most "crownings" wins.

Losers—better luck next Leap Year.

Skin the Goat

This game follows the same illogical pattern, except that the nag, pony, or goat is made up of only a pillow and one back. The first runner tries to crown the pillow while the back resorts to a rodeo performance that would stop anything short of a Sherman Tank. If the back bucks the runner, the runner limps into line, adding another link to the ever-growing, angry goat. If by chance someone does crown the pillow, he becomes the next pillow -- but the chances of that are remote. The world goat record is 195 links.

Meter Leap Frog

All the players line up at one end of a block which is lined with parking meters. Since Carl Magee invented the meter, first installed in Oklahoma City during the summer of 1935, kids around the country have made this a favorite vaulting pastime. It is played among teen-agers who have the height and strength to clear the meters without losing their sexual identity.

Two Deep

In this circle chase, all but two players face inward as backs. A runner and chaser start the game on opposite sides of the circle. The runner is chased around the circle and can only save his skin by leaping over a back into the circle. That back immediately becomes the next runner and the ex-runner a back. Tagging changes a runner into the chaser. It's an exciting game of constant transformation.

Jump Rope

ORIGIN:

Jumping with a rope or grape vine followed children skipping to rhymes, songs, and ballads. Many of the old ballads and chants have been passed down through the centuries, the most popular ones from England and Germany. Today there are over 3,000 recorded chants alone.

RULES:

There are no formalized rules in jump rope, and the key to starting a group game is deciding quickly who is first ender.* Everyone volunteers for the job.

There are several types of jumps:

For one person:

Double Jumps -- two skips between each turn of the rope.

Single (Hot Pepper) -- one skip for every turn of the rope.

Criss-Cross -- the rope is criss-crossed on every turn before the jump is made.

Backward -- the rope is turned in the opposite direction of single or double jumping.

For three or more people:

Double Dutch -- two long ropes simultaneously going in opposite directions (used for group jumping). A 200 year old import from the Dutch.

Hot Pepper -- fast turn of the rope, allowing one skip between each turn.

> *I'm a little Dutch girl dressed in blue.*
> *These are the things I like to do.*
> *Salute to the captain, curtsy to the queen,*
> *And turn my back on the mean old king.*

* see Glossary

VARIATION:

Chinese Jump Rope

Draw a box on the ground (or use sidewalk squares). Start with the rope six inches from the ground, over the center of the box. The first person jumps over the rope and out the other side of the box, then (for the sake of new vistas) back again in the opposite direction. If the player touches the rope, he's out.

The rope should be raised two inches each time the jumper jumps, until the rope is too high to jump any more without touching it, at which point it's the turn of the next player.

Dolly Dimple throws a kiss.
Dolly Dimple misses like this (stop the rope with left foot)

Bluebells, cockleshells
  Eevey, ivey, over.
  Here come the teacher with a big fat stick.
  You'd better learn your arithmetic.
  1 and 1 are two.
  2 and 2 are four.
  Now it's time for spelling.
  1 and 1 makes 2
  D O G spells dog.
  Now it's time for math.
  1 and 1 makes 2
  2 and 1 makes 3.
  2 and 2 makes 4.
  Come on lass and skip some more.
  4 minus 1 makes 3.
  3 minus 1 makes 2.
  2 minus 1 makes 1.
  Now our arithmetic is done.

Apples, peaches, pears and plums,
  Tell me when your birthday comes.
  (chant months until your birthday, and then days until your birthday)

Changing in the bedroom,
  One by one, two by two, etc.
  (Each time an additional player jumps in until someone misses)

Tarzan, Tarzan, in the air.
  Tarzan lost his underwear.
  Tarzan say, me no care.
  Jane find me new underwear.
  (Jane, boy, cheetah may be substituted
  for Tarzan, and the last line
  becomes "me no wear no underwear")

Ma-bel Ma-bel set the ta-ble "close the door when you are a-ble Ten Twenty Thirty etc.

Not last night,
but the night before.
24 robbers came knocking at my door.
As I went out (hop up and turn around once),
To let them come back in,
This is what I heard them say,
Spanish dancer do the splits (spread legs),
The kicks, the turn arounds,
The touch the grounds,
Get out of town (and jump out).
Spanish dancer please come back.
Sit on a tack,
Read a book but please don't look.
(Close your eyes and wait for the rope
to wrap around your ankle or neck)

I scream,
You scream,
We all scream
For ice cream.

Roses are red,
Violets are blue,
I like pecans,
Nuts to you.

Had a little girl dressed in blue;
She died last night at half past two,
Did she go up or down?
"Up," "down," "up," "down," etc.

Cinderella, dressed in yella,
Went downtown to buy some jello.
On the way her girdle busted.
How many people were disgusted?
1, 2, 3, 4, etc.
      or
Cinderelli, dressed in yelli,
Went upstairs to kiss a felli.
Made a mistake and kissed a snake.
How many doctors did it take?
1, 2, 3, 4, etc. (until you miss)

Teddy bear, Teddy bear, turn around.
Teddy bear, Teddy bear, touch the ground.
Teddy bear, Teddy bear, go upstairs.
Teddy bear, Teddy bear, say your prayers
Teddy bear, Teddy bear, say goodnight
Teddy bear, Teddy bear, turn out the light, etc.

Policeman, policeman, do your duty.
Here comes Sally, an American beauty.
She can wiggle, she can waggle.
She can do the twist.
I bet you ten dollars,
That she can't do this.
Turn around, touch the ground,
Get out of town.

Touch  Tag Football

ORIGIN:

Football has it's footing in two Greek games of the past. *Harpastrum,* the first, is an ancient game in which two opposing sides seized and randomly ran away from each other with the ball. *Epikoinos* had a dissimilar, even contradictory, playing pattern from Harpastrum. The ball was placed on a line, and each team tried to kick it over its opponent's goal line. But the two games married, and a new diversion -- Throw and Kick -- was born. The Romans at the height of the Empire, the Italians during the Renaissance, the English under the reign of Elizabeth, all played the wild game on a playground that was miles wide and miles long, often driving the ball between vying villages along the countryside. This fiasco raised fighting to festive proportions within a playing field bounded only by the limits and obstacles of Mother Nature.

Through the centuries, the name of Throw and Kick applied more frequently to bodily contact than to the ball. Self-restraint was nonexistent and, in fact, the game lacked any control whatever until the Victorian days. The Victorians dignified the game, transferring the quaint practice of kicking, hitting, punching, throwing, wrestling, and generally mutilating the players to exercising these aggressions on the ball. The robust days of sublimating in Kick and Throw were over. The wooden ball was shelved by the English, and Rugby, with a softer ball, came into its day. Rugby further curbed bickering, fractures, and black eyes into the rough, but mannered, sport of Football.

Football played in the 1700's at the market place.

Finally, more modification came about when the sport hit the streets. The asphalt, a less-than-silken surface, was incompatible with the flesh of tackled bodies. The body absorbed the shock while leaving the gutter intact, and most of the body in the gutter. To alleviate this problem, "tag" or "touch" was substituted for the "tackle" as the

Yale football team 1894

safer way to stop the opponent. (Tripping, though, still worked pretty well.) In addition to the gutter problem, the impact between a running player and a parked car was forceful enough to stop him momentarily--three days at the most.

Some of the street games we play at Gilmore City Iowa.
The boys often play Kill it is a football game that everyone is against everyone.

Emily Benjamin
Age 10

The featherweight Right Half holding the ball is Serling at age six. Note the aggressive determination explicit even in those days.

Cordially,

Rod Serling

EQUIPMENT:
    1 football
    chalk to mark off the goal lines

OBJECTIVE:
    To carry and advance the ball over the opposing team's goal line.

RULES:
The rules of Touch Football and Tackle Football are essentially the same except that the substitution of touching the person carrying the ball has eliminated sending him nose first to the street as with tackling.

One team kicks the oval-shaped ball to its opponents. Once the ball is caught, the kickers run toward their opponents, blocking and pushing them aside. The carriers make a valiant team effort, in the face of this hostility, to get the ball as close to the adversary's goal as possible without being tagged. Unfortunately, the team relies on individual stardom and confusion (which is the most common strategy).

When the ball carrier is tagged, the ball is placed in the middle of the street parallel to the tagging spot. This is called the "first down." There are only four downs in street Football, after which the ball switches sides. The team that has the ball goes into a huddle to discuss strategy. The Captain gets a rock and draws out the plan on the street or, if he fears the other team is microfilming his ingenious play, he uses a stick to make imaginary lines on the pavement. Once no one understands what is going on, the huddle breaks up, each member throwing his hands in the air, shouting an unintelligible cheer. Actually, it is more of a moan in unison which sets the playing spirit in motion.

One person throws the ball to the quarterback after the appropriate signal, and the quarterback, usually the captain, recites the complicated call: "strawberries, pickles 1, 2, 7, 9; ink, blink, the teachers stink, 4, 6; bottles, sticks, 12, 5 ... hike," before receiving the ball on the word "hike." The quarterback gets the ball, and the opposing team counts out loud to ten in three seconds flat. Then they rush him.

During this counted moment of repose, the quarterback quickly decides what to do since no one on the field has followed his plan. They're all out there pointing to themselves or discretely yelling "Me, Me" for a pass. The quarterback can only pass the ball forward or run with it himself. If the ball is intercepted on the former option, the opposing team gets the ball at that point. If the carrying team, however, is only four feet from their own goal by the third down, chances are good that they will either kick the ball -- or quit the game altogether.

On the upbeat, however, the carrier who successfully takes the ball over the opposing goal without being tagged, scores a touchdown. Each team alternates the ball after each touchdown or fourth down.

SPECIAL WORDS OF INTEREST:

Scrimmage: This is the line where the opposing teams line up and face each other during the "down." The line is defined by where the ball carrier was tagged.

Lateral pass: Passing the ball to a fellow player who is to the side rather than in front of him.

Penalties: If a penalty is called, the ball goes back several feet. A foot is defined as the length of a player's shoe (that of whomever has the biggest foot).

SCORING:

Every touchdown is worth six points. Whichever team has the greater number of points at the end of the game wins.

VARIATIONS:

Razzle-Dazzle

All the rules of Tag Football remain intact except that the ball can be passed backward, laterally, and forward as many times as the team wishes during a single down. If the ball is dropped, it is dead, and the line of scrimmage is where the ball was last thrown.

Football in the 1500's.

LVDVS QVEM ITALI·APPELLANT·IL CALCIO

Flag

Again, the same as Touch, except that a shirt or rag is stuffed into each player's pants. Instead of tagging, the flag must be pulled out in order to stop the action.

Powder-Puff

Mocking chauvinism, the women played ball and the men cheered:

Ra Ra Ree,
Kick him in the knee.
Ra Ra Rass,
Kick him in the other knee.

But with today's liberation, everyone plays ball.

Hopscotch

18th Century engraving

ORIGIN:

The word "scotch" in Hopscotch refers to a stone, one essential part of the game. The other significant element is the diagram. The history of the diagram has many conflicting theories, but there is some general agreement about its symbolism dating to the early years of Christianity. The idea that the myth of the labyrinths in ancient times stimulated the original game has been suggested.

During the Christian era, Hopscotch was most probably derived from a combination of the earlier games and reconstructed along eschatological lines of the Church. The game might represent the journey of the human soul from earth to heaven or the strata in the Kingdom of God, where man's position is defined in the hierarchy as in Pope's "Essay on Man". The former theory seems to prevail, in which the last, or uppermost, square is heaven or everlasting glory. One scholar carried it further and suggested that the heathen labyrinth, an allegorical figure of heaven, was replaced with a form duplicating the Basilicon. The Christian Church, like the diagram, was divided into seven parts, where paradise, the inner sanctuary of heaven, was the altar, the inner heart of the church.

In this form, the game was popular in England during the 17th century, before it voyaged to America with the early settlers. The early church diagram is still the most popular one drawn, though there are variations in some countries. Likewise, there are many different names, though Hopscotch and Potsy prevail, particularly in the United States. Potsy was probably derived from the word "potshot," which means to shoot casually at an easy target.

OBJECT:
> To project a stone onto a linearly marked-off diagram on the street or dirt and hop in specific patterns without touching any of the lines.

GENERAL RULES:

Diagram or Court
This is outlined with chalk on a pavement or with a stick on the ground.

Stone or Puck
The traditional game is played with a flat stone, such as that used for "skipping" over water; but in cities where stones are not easily found, a rubber heel makes an admirable substitute.

The Play
This consists of hopping or jumping into the different sections of the diagram and out again in a prescribed manner and order, with or without playing a stone (puck). In all hopping games it is amiss to change the hopping foot during any given play, or to touch the other foot or any part of the person to the ground, except where the game calls for that, as in straddling. It is also amiss to touch a line with the hopping foot.

Straddling consists of jumping to a stride position in two spaces, one foot on each side of the line. Straddling is usually in the nature of a rest from hopping, as the weight may not only be on both feet, but the feet in some games are allowed to rest wholly on the ground unless "toes only" is specified. Jumping (both feet together) is subject to the same rules as hopping in not touching lines or ground.

Throwing and Kicking Stone (Puck)
When the stone is thrown it must land wholly within the space intended; for it to touch or cross a line is a miss. When it is kicked out it must always go out over the base or end lines and not over the side lines.

The stone may be shoved by the hopping foot to a more advantageous position within its square or space before being kicked out. The player may hop around in this space as much as he pleases before, during, or after touching the stone, so long as he observes all rules about not touching lines or ground. To throw the stone or puck, the player must stand outside the

As a child in New York, I did play a lot of hop scotch, and also roller skated in Central Park on two wheel roller skates. I haven't seen any of these since.

All best wishes,

Dina Merrill

baseline and in most games must be in a hopping position when making the throw. He may bend forward, but must not touch the lines or ground within them with his foot or any part of his person.

Players

They are not limited as to numbers. They take turns in regular order. Any player missing gives way at once to the next player; when his turn comes around again he begins by playing over the particular play on which he missed, unless otherwise specified, as in part of the Italian game. All players begin with the first play, or stunt, unless otherwise directed, as in the English game in which a player begins with the play on which the previous player failed. It is a miss also to a) play out of turn, b) make the wrong play.

Winning

The player wins who has gone through the entire game with the fewest number of turns (misses), everyone else having played. That is, if he should be fortunate enough to play the entire series without a miss, he has not won until every other player has had his turn and missed.

Italian Hopscotch
Read General Rules, first.

(See diagram on following page)

a. Throw puck or stone into spaces 1 through 7, successively, and into the end space marked *Rest,* being careful that the stone doesn't land in the blank spaces.

b. At each throw, hop on one foot into spaces 1, 4, and 7, and straddle on toes, spaces 2/3 and 5/6. Omit the two blank spaces and the space containing the puck, by hopping over them.

c. Land on *Rest* on both feet flat on the ground, and jump to reverse the position of feet. Retrace the steps, stopping to pick up the stone.

d. If the stone lands in the middle blank space, the player loses his turn and must begin on the next turn from the space he played before the bad toss. If the stone lands in the farthest blank space, however, the penalty is even harder -- he not only loses his turn, but must also start again from box 1.

VARIATION: *Sky Blue*

Expert players may enhance their achievement by hopping and straddling (without playing the puck) through the diagram with eyes shut.

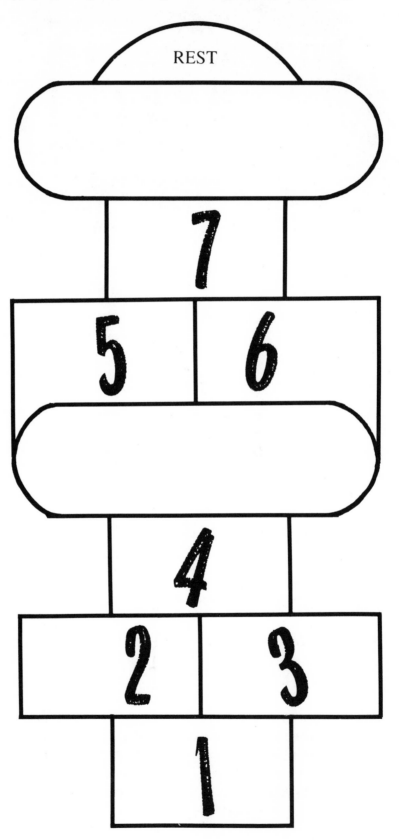

Six Variations of
French Hopscotch (Marraine)

7

Stunt No. 1--Houses

Throw the stone, while standing outside the baseline, into any square -- or let it land where it may. That square becomes the thrower's "house," in which his initials are written. Thereafter, the owner of the house may rest on both feet in that box, but all other players must hop over it.

8

The game becomes increasingly difficult as each player has the privilege of taking a house after completing a series, thus setting aside more and more squares in which the players may not set foot.

6

Stunt No. 2

a. Throw the stone into square 1.
b. Hop into that square, kicking the stone, with small hops on the hopping foot, into square 2.

4

c. Hop into 2, and in the same way send the stone into square 3, and so on, through the diagram and back, always hopping on the same foot. Double squares are hopped in numbered order, not straddled.
d. It is a miss if the stone stops on a line.

5

Stunt No. 3

Instead of throwing the stone, place it on the back of an outstretched hand, and hop and straddle through the entire diagram and back again without the stone falling off.

3

Stunt No. 4

Same, with the stone on the head.

2

Stunt No. 5

Same, with the stone held on the toe of the hopping foot.

1

Stunt No. 6

Hop through and back without the stone, but with the eyes shut.

I Hop Scotch is a Game i Like to play

l. age 7.

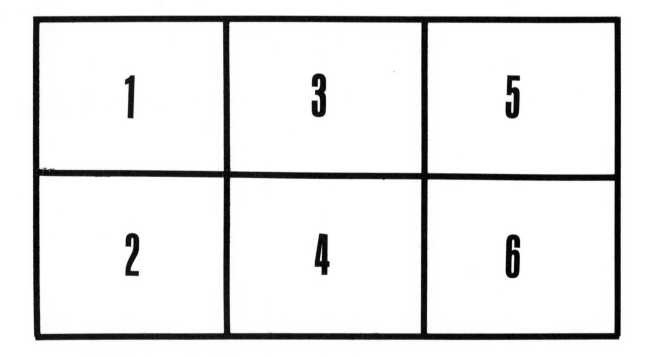

1	3	5
2	4	6

English Hopscotch

Each player jumps through the squares with the stone between his sneakers or shoes. He must jump like a kangaroo -- one hop-jump to a square. A miss, or drop of the stone, forfeits the turn to the next player.

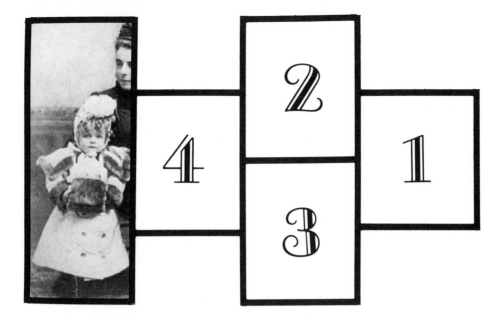

Snail Hopscotch

Played without a puck or stone, the player hops on one foot through the diagram (one hop to a space) until reaching the center space marked *Rest,* where both feet may be put on the ground. The hopping is then reversed to the outside space and then out.

When a player has done this, he writes his initials on any space he may choose, except *Rest,* (a variation on House) -- where he may rest on both feet, while the other players must hop over the landowner's space -- still on one foot.

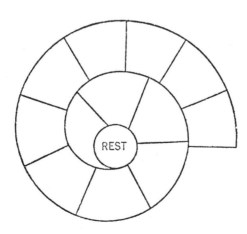

Stare, Blinking, and Silence

ORIGIN:

Though no date can be affixed to this game, one can assume that people have been staring at each other for a very long time. There are such inferences even in the story of Adam and Eve.

OBJECTIVE:

One of the three games, Blinking, involves the involuntary nervous system, while the other two rely on the voluntary system. In all three, the overall goal is for one player to wait out his opponent or make him do an overt rather than subtle act (as compared to King of the Mountain, Chestnuts, Knuckles, etc.) within a specified time limit -- before he blows it himself.

RULES:

Staring or Stare Down

Two opponents face each other (which is a very accurate description in this game). They make sullen faces, half smirks, pretend to be on the verge of

.063 seconds

.064 seconds

.066 seconds

.067 seconds

.069 seconds

.071 seconds

cracking up, spread their cheeks, stick out their tongues -- all in an effort to break each other's stare. Eventually, a slight smile and giggle creeps out, followed by a burst of laughter, breaking the stalemate. During the match, no player can talk to or touch his opponent. It is strictly the art of one glum face psyching out another. The steadiest sourpuss wins the game.

Blinking

This facial game works independently of will or determination. Those who suffer from anxiety or who have eye ticks or twitches (or hate the thought of eye drops) are sure losers. Two challengers face each other and hold their eyes wide open. Shaking the blinking impulse requires great concentration. Unfortunately, this concentration is the same as thinking about not swallowing, which only makes one feel more like swallowing. The more one "thinks," the greater the urge to swallow--or, as in this case, blink. The brain struggles against the determined eyelids' urge to shut tight for a moment's relief. The eyes begin to water and one player's defeat is a tear away. The game can be played with more than two people if there are enough judges to watch the contestants (without tearing themselves).

Silence

This test of mandibular control fortifies the thought that "silence is golden." Two or more players sit in a circle and remain quiet as long as possible. Whenever the silence is broken, the noisemaker is eliminated from the contest. The first to break the silence is branded a monkey's uncle (great practice for the silent majority). The final mute wins.

VARIATION:

One person keeps time while a player attempts to remain silent in the face of jeering, badgering friends who try to stir a reaction. Again, there can be no physical contact.

In an even more complex variation, motionlessness is added to silence. The person who spends the most time in a vegetable state holds the street title.

Parents encourage these games while spending an extended period of time with their children -- particularly in restaurants and on long car rides. (If that doesn't work, listing car makes, brands of cigarettes, or identifying license plates holds most kids for an hour or two. In the evening, it's Search for Padidlies -- cars with one headlight out -- that holds bedlam back.)

S t r e t c h

ORIGIN:

This daring duel of knives is a vicarious descendent of mumbly-peg.

EQUIPMENT:

2 players
1 knife (preferably a sheath or Bowie knife named after the legendary Jim Bowie.)

OBJECT:

To force the enemy to stretch his legs as far apart as possible till the victim is immobile, or has collapsed.

RULES:

Whatever the psychologists say about young people sublimating through play, there can be no mistake about Stretch. Stretch players are hostile. In addition to repressed hostility, each player must have a dismal sense of reality, strong nerve, and an unchivalrous orientation. In certain stages of

development, that doesn't exclude many people. One rarely notices any fear of danger or concern on the part of the players for themselves or for each other. Only the game is in the forefront of their minds.

The two competitors, with their feet tightly squeezed together, stand facing each other about a yard apart. One player throws the knife from the blade to the left or right of his adversary's shoes. The throw cannot land more than one foot from the side of his opponent's shoe.

After the shot, the human target moves the foot closest to the blade to the point of entry. He removes the knife and returns the throw from his new standing position. The throwing and stretching process alternates between the daredevils. No player is required to move his feet if the knife doesn't stick in the ground (even the whimpering knife which goes in but slowly droops to the ground falls into this category) or if it is overshot in excess of a foot from the foot.

No matter how many incomplete plays there are, the eventual truth is that the players can only spread their legs so far. Even if they can still reach or throw the knife, one of them is bound to fall over, ending the game.

There is a slight change of rules which can indefinitely lengthen an otherwise short bout. Luckily for lads, this game has its prime before they discover the existence or need of the athletic supporter. Should one player be straining his thigh muscles and the other player be still in a position recognizably human, the advantaged player can throw the knife between his opponent's suffering legs -- in the ground, of course. This is called splitting, and a successful split means that the thrower can bring his legs back together again. Then he is in a great position to kill his foe. This timely choice of splitting is open to each player no matter how far gone he may be. Generally, both players try to limit the number of splits executed in a game or the match could well go on till puberty.

Closies or Chicken

This game, lurid and lively, is the reverse of Stretch, requiring skill and stupidity. Each player starts the match with his legs wide apart. Watching players groan and struggle, maximizing the spread of their legs is in itself a spectator sport.

One player throws the knife between his opponents' legs. The target moves his shoe to the blade. Alternating turns, the shooting range narrows with each shot. This demands superb aim from the thrower and iron nerves from the target.

The claustrophobia of the feet continues until the narrow boundaries cause one player to question the dueling abilities of his opponent or until he reveres the sanctity of his own flesh. Detente or no, there is never a stalemate in Stretch. One person must bow out and be proclaimed "chicken" or risk the nightmare of Macbeth -- "Oh, bloody dagger!"

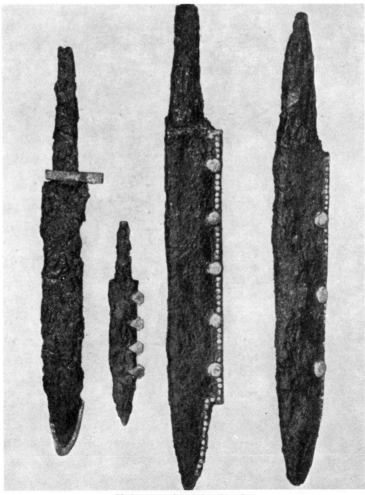

Knives used by the Franks.

King of the Mountain

ORIGIN:

King of the Mountain or Castle is not depicted until the mid-16th century (then as *Blockhuis*, or *De berg is myn*). But, the game has been around as long as there have been power struggles between men.

OBJECTIVE:

To remove the man at the top and take his place. "Survival of the fittest."

RULES:

Here the rules are rather flexible and border on organized savagery. The game is most often played on a pile of dirt or on top of a stoop or car.

One man, for no known reason (and the game lacks any semblance of reason), rushes to the top position and declares:

I'm the king of the castle,
And you're the dirty rascal.

This is no way to talk to the populace, nor does it show much benevolence for a newly non-elected official. Needless to say, this provokes the wrath of the ruled.

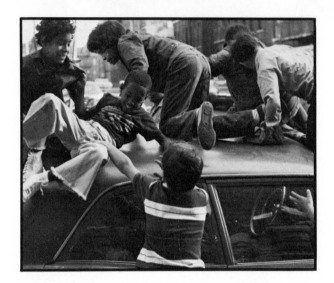

There can be no peaceful settlement by negotiation since the subjects are equally power hungry.

An uprising takes place, there is the battle cry, "ah-ooo-ga," then it's a matter of who can pull down the self-proclaimed leader by pulling his ankles, punching his legs, or plain wrestling to force his downfall. Regardless, the king, keeping in character, claims executive privilege and proceeds to kick his opponents in the head. He will fight for his god-given right to protect the kingship (kingdency) until someone stronger pulls him down. Power to the people.

Once the king has been overthrown, the new leader claims his rights and proceeds to enforce the same domestic policies as his predecessor, which are hardly domestic (for that matter hardly civilized). It's just a matter of time before another coup takes place, each leader taking the beating that comes with such grave responsibility as leadership.

The rules have barely changed over the centuries, reinforcing the civic lesson that "the system does work."

This was supposed to have been the favorite game of Napoleon.

THE NEW KID

One spring day, the pollen count skyrockets and a new family moves onto the block. The children of the new family are mentioned only by number and gender -- three boys, two girls, etc. They must act bravely before the block council and mold themselves into the established conformities of the neighborhood. Their acknowledgment and acceptance hinges on this.

The childhood of man is a closed brotherhood, rarely entered into by "new" people. The new kid is always greeted with curiosity and suspicion. He must prove himself, and thus be deemed worthy of the street's friendship. (Dreadful as the thought is, some remain "new" kids even after having resided on the block for 12 years). The "new" kid is anxious to lose his stigma of "new-ness," and become "used" (as indeed he will be).

In some of the less fortunate cases of "new" kids, mother spends her first day telling her "new" neighbors that her son Benny makes friends so easily and is sensitive and mature—in fact, she claims, "He's been a teenager since he's three." Right away this kid is in trouble. No matter what mother wants, or how she sees it, it is the new kid who must adapt to the majority value system. It's street life -- he must live with it and live it. Mothers with intervention tendencies make their child's life with the group only more difficult.

The following represents a series of physical/emotional tests, determining bravery, endurance, humility, character, etc. The new kid must pass these before initiation into the family that is only held together by a name or number on a small street sign.

NEW KID TRAINING PROGRAM AND EXAMINATION

PART I: PERSONAL INTERVIEW
1. Do you like girls? Boys?
2. Do you like your teacher?
3. How many sewers can you hit? (See Stickball.)
4. Can you keep a secret? (Must swear never to tell parents about these proceedings.)
5. Do you know how to play 52-Pick-Up?

PART II: ENDURANCE
The block members prepare to apply the principle of all against one in *Run the Gauntlet*. Ten or twelve happy little beavers line themselves up, one behind the other, each with his legs spread apart. The victimized individual (or testee) crawls through the tunnel of legs. Each member forming this Tunnel of Love smacks, bites, pinches, or punches the newcomer as he goes through. This he must do, without shedding one tear, if he is to be accepted and if he wants to be accepted. Crybabies are out.

PART III: OBEDIENCE AND MUSICAL TACKINESS

Educational Doctrine

(Tune: The Marine Hymn)

> *From the Halls of Montezuma*
> *To the shores of PTA*
> *We will fight our teacher's battle,*
> *With spitballs and with clay.*
> *We will fight for more recess,*
> *And to keep our desks a mess, (dirty mess!-shout)*
> *We are proud to claim the title*
> *Of teachers little pests. Hey!*

(The content of the song falls along the lines of other great hymns like "Mine eyes have seen the glory of the burning of the school".)

Culinary Doctrine

During lunch the new kid must listen and then—*bon apetit!*

(Tune - The Old Grey Mare)

> *Great big gobs of greasy, grimy, gopher guts,*
> *Mutilated monkey meat,*
> *Little birdies' dirty feet, (or petrified piggy's feet)*
> *Top it all off with pulverized vulture beaks*
> *Oops! I forgot my spoon.*

During the encore, the new kid is watched carefully. If he doesn't throw up by the song's end, he has manners and taste that make him acceptable.

PART IV: REFLEX AND CLEVERNESS

One member of the in-group points to a button on the kid's shirt. As the kid looks down, the pointing hand swiftly moves up, slapping the face. Taking advantage of a kid's good nature or innocence is the greatest pleasure for some blockbullies. Such antagonists have little to lose or risk by such challenge—in fact, are just as glad if the kid fails and the tightly-knit group remains unaltered.

The 3rd Quarter

BRUEGHEL: *CHILDREN'S GAMES*

Capture the Flag
Stickball, Wiffle® Ball, Punchball,
  Slapball, Halfball
Chestnuts
Bottle Snatch or Steal the Bacon
Red Rover
Coins—Flipping, Trading,
  Hitting, Pitching
Pussy Wants a Corner or Puss-Puss
Hydrants
Johnny on the Pony or Buck-Buck
Mother May I? or Giant Steps
Flies Up, Kickball, and Tip-Cat
Statues
Kick the Can
Running Bases
Simon Says
Flinch
Pom-Pom Pullaway

SAFETY AND THE LAW

rueghel

1. Playing with dolls	45. Pyramid building and lifting
2. Jacks (kuncklebones)	46. Carrying loaf of bread
3. Rattles	47. Fly swatting
4. Windmill toy (whirligig)	48. Keep Away (Saluggi)
5. Blowing bubbles	49. Fisherman cord game
6. Playing with pet animal	50. The fish
7. Piggy back ride	51. Bowling (Bocci)
8. Processional	52. Throwing knucklebones (jacks)
9. Hand seat carrying	53. Walking on High Stilts
10. Riding hobby horse	54. Hanging on fence
11. Playing fife and drum	55. Piggy Back
12. Making mud pies	56. Spinning tops
13. Hoops	57. Spinning tops
14. Looking down cask hole	58. Drop the Handkerchief
15. Hoop with bells	59. Spinning around
16. Barreling	60. King of the Mountain
17. Inflating animal skin (forrunner to blowing up balloons)	61. Swings
	62. Swimming
18. Buck Buck or Saddle the Nag	63. Wading (skinny dipping)
19. Playing Store	64. Mulberry Bush
20. Building castles	65. Climbing a tree
21. Pulling hair (Haarken Plunken)	66. Taw (marbles)
22. Pull and heave	67. "Time out"
23. Leapfrog	68. Flag waving (streamers)
24. Tug of War (chicken fight position)	69. Bombardment (forrunner to water balloon warfare)
25. Run the Gauntlet	
26. Odds or Evens (choosing sides)	70. Balancing a broom
27. Blindman's Bluff	71. Hitting stones
28. Hide and Seek	72. Cord game
29. Somersaults (tumbling)	73. Taw (marbles)
30. Pop gun	74. Bottoms-Up (Potch in Tuchis)
31. Playing Church and Clergy	75. Procession
32. Masks	76. Hunt the Fox (Hound and Hare)
33. Digging Ditches	77. Wrestling
34. Climbing on a fence	78. Climbing a wall
35. Jousting with windmills	79. Annoyed innkeeper
36. Cartwheeling	80. Follow the Leader
37. Doing a headstand	81. Playing doorkeeper
38. Playing with rattle	82. Doctor
39. Playing on fence	83. Horsey (shoulder ride)
40. Procession (wedding)	84. Tag
41. Selling apples	85. Pushing girl off beam
42. Delightful noise-banging an iron pot (early inspiration to Kick the Can)	86. Play pretending (myth of the lengendary magical horse)
	87. Marching
43. Make-believe fishing	*Painted in 1560*
44. Walking on short stilts	

Street Games   141

Capture the Flag

ORIGIN:

This game, in its own disorganized fashion, is a take-off on the raids between the English and Scottish borders. Raids and the game were a regular pastime in England in a period when the American colonies were declaring independence from the mother country. Not long after the Revolution, American kids were playing this English carry-over.

EQUIPMENT:

2 flags (or shirts of different colors)

OBJECT:

One team tries to capture the opposing team's flag and return safely with the flag. (A good promoter of hate and war.)

RULES:

In its newest form, the rules are quite clear. But as in all wars, interpreting what's fair while under attack adds dimension, cunning, and zest to the rules of the play.

The group is divided into two teams and the block is divided into two zones, sides, or countries, depending on how seriously the game is to be taken. The line of demarcation is designated by scraping with a rock across the asphalt if a piece of chalk is unavailable. At the end of the war zones, the flag (or article of clothing) is hung in open view. In some cases, this is revolting and a cause for any declaration of war. In addition to the flag being raised, imaginary jails are built near the flag, and one member of each team is chosen to be jailkeeper.

Team captains or generals plan strategies, dividing their teams into offensive and defensive units. The defenders stay behind the line of demarcation to protect their flag from invaders. The offenders who invade the foreign soil are hefty aggressors, capable runners, and, in general, rather offensive individuals.

Each team sends its attacking unit into the opposing territory to capture the enemy flag. Sometimes the approach incorporates shrewd subterfuge, but more often it's a massive force play rushing the defense. Those guarding the flag are empowered to tag, hold, or tackle invaders within their territory. The only way to count a fallen victim a prisoner is to shout "caught" three times while pouncing on his body. This is where the real hand-to-hand combat begins. A good punch in the nose tends to end any prolonged scuffle.

Once someone from the invading force has been captured, he is taken off to jail, where he remains for the rest of the game unless some sly member of his team sneaks through enemy lines to help him escape. The hero runs into the prison, shouting, "Free, free, free," and the bust is a success. It is the job of the jailkeeper to guard the prison against such heroic figures.

The game is carried to various degrees, often involving offensives, decoys, binoculars, counter-offensives, etc., and can run the full course of a day. Team casualties fluctuate, heightening the suspense of the final outcome. Hopefully, the balance tips severely in one team's favor. This "most favored nation" status enables the so endowed to send in one or more special troops with decoys to snatch the flag and successfully return home without any of the opposing side wrapped around their ankles in a valiant last effort.

If the tactic works, the flag comes over the lines, the conquered defense forces sink into the dirt, and peace is at hand. Overall, full-scale activity of this sort gives opportunity for such brutal and futile combat that even John Wayne would have to admire.

Stickball, Kickball, Wiffle® Ball, Punchball, Slapball, Halfball

ORIGIN:

Though baseball, the national sport of the United States, is the modern forefather of Stickball, its true roots lie in two English games of the late 18th century. The first of these, Old Cat, was played with bases, a bat, and a ball. The batter hit the ball and ran between the bases and home plate repeatedly, until the ball was returned by the outfielder.

The other game, Rounders, was played on a rectangular field, delineated by four eighteen-inch sticks, the fourth of these being the home stick. Again, it was a race against the ball being returned by the outfield.

The early settlers brought both these games with them, bringing Town Ball to the New World. (It was frequently played by relaxing soldiers in Boston during the Revolution but called Stool-ball). The game was well on its way to stardom by the early 1800's, and the birth of the broken window was not far behind.

At about the same time, 1798 to be exact, Theodore Bates, a Shaker from Watervliet, New York, invented the first flat broom. His invention rose in popularity along with baseball and the handle became the most widely used bat in cities across the nation.

By 1839, a colonel in the army, Abner Doubleday, solidified Town Ball and Rounders into Baseball. He drew the first diamond and defined fielding positions. He also eliminated the practice of throwing the ball at the runner to put (or knock) him out (as the case may be).

In 1845, the first official rules were drawn up by the Knickerbocker Club of New York. During the Civil War, it was the most popular game of the Yanks and slowly migrated south with the enthusiastic rebels. Today, without war and behavior less than civil, city kids play an adapted baseball in the streets with the aid of the product of Theodore Bates' genius. The only tradition that remains from Colonial Town Ball is the broken window.

EQUIPMENT:

1 spaldeen

1 piece of chalk

1 broomstick without the broom (wrapping adhesive tape around one end of the stick makes for a better grip)

RULES:

The bat method of choosing sides is used. The ideal setup is two teams, each with five players. The sewer closest to the intersection is designated as home plate. First and third base are the fifth car parked by the curb to the left and right of the sewer, respectively. A chalked "X" by the rear tire of the car pinpoints the base. Second base is the second manhole from the intersection in the middle of the street.

The ball can be pitched in or it can be thrown up and hit by the batter, himself. In the latter case, he stands on home base, throws the ball into the air, and hits it on the fly or a bounce. This is called "hitting fungo." The fielders react differently to each hitter -- they will move farther out into the field if the batter is a long hitter, or "sewer socker" (can hit more than two sewers).

Righty or lefty, each time the batter misses the ball, it's a strike. Three strikes and the batter steps down and is out. There are no balls called in the game. Once the broomstick makes contact with the pinky, or spaldeen, the ball can take one of several courses.

The ball is in play if it is hit within the field or goes beyond first and third base, whether or not it hits a building, car, or sidewalk. However, the batter is out if the ball goes over a roof beyond first and third, bounces off a building, and is caught, or if it is caught on a fly within the field. The player who hits a ball that hits a car, hydrant, lamppost (or a passerby) calls "hindu." In the West, South and North, it is called interference, or "do-over," and the ball is put into play again. (The term "hindu" is not connected with any Far-Eastern religion, but most likely stems from the word hinderance. Kids, always searching for nicknames, probably shortened the term to the abbreviated hinder, which in time became Brooklyn-ized to hindu.)

Any ball hit far down the street and past the fielders is closely followed by the batter running after his own long shot. If the spaldeen survives being walloped by the stick, the game lasts nine innings as in Baseball.

Some cities with congested streets, particularly Philadelphia and Boston, prefer the ball split in half to be played as Halfball. If there are no pinkeys to be ripped in half, a piece of rubber hosing is often substituted.

Stick ball was a game which had all the rules of baseball modified to some small degree. It was played with a high-bounce rubber ball. It could be played with a pitcher or the batter could pitch to himself by simply throwing the ball up and hitting it. The bat was a stick, usually the rod part of a mop or a broom. The game was played on the streets. We made bases by drawing them in with a chalk and there was a great deal of excitement because one never knew when one would break a window or when the police would come because stick ball was an illegal game since many windows were broken. The thrill, the joy, the satisfaction of making contact with a high-bounce Spalding and letting it fly three sewers, which was about 300 ft., was incomparable to anything that I know of today. Also, leaping up a brownstone and climbing on the railing of the stoop and almost going as high as the first story to pull down a fly ball with the bases loaded was another extra-ordinarily joyful moment.

That's about it.

Sincerely,

Walter Matthau

My favorite games are golf, chewing gum and baseball.

Jerry Lewis

My favorite sports were baseball and swimming.

Sincerely yours,

Sam J. Ervin, Jr.

I'm sorry to say that the only games I've ever been interested in are indoor games, although I have a vague memory of playing stickball in the street when I was a kid. At any rate, there are certainly no photographs.

Yours sincerely,

Stephen Sondheim

Right: Lyndon Johnson playing ball on the prairie.

SCORING:

A score box is drawn, one horizontal line intersecting nine short verticals (on the sidewalk or street). An unbiased scorekeeper fills in the runs each team makes at the end of each inning -- under the scrutiny of the captains. The team with the most runs at the end of the nine innings wins the game. The only exception is in the case of a tie score when extra innings are played until the team with the "last licks" scores the breaking point.

rotten apples |1 |0 |0 |0 |1 |2
mean mamas (us) |0 |0 |3 |1 |0 |1

LINGO:

Foul-tip -- Batter tips the ball behind him.
Chips -- Retail value of the ball.
Bunt -- Tapping the ball.
Grounder -- A ball hit along the gutter as opposed to a fly ball.
Sacrifice -- Batter hits a single or flies out, in effect sacrificing himself
     to let another runner on third base reach home sewer, scoring a run.

VARIATIONS:

Punchball

Instead of smashing the pinky with a broomstick, the fist or open hand (Slapball) is substituted, but one's sewer skill remains. All the rules of Stickball apply. Kickball also follows the same rules -- except that a large red ball is kicked. The ball can be punched in or kicked fungo.

Triangle

This is the version of Punchball for a limited number of players. There is no second base and the ball is pitched in (unlike Punchball). In fact, the ball must bounce in the batter's circle before it can be punched (see diagram); otherwise, the rules of Stickball apply.

The game I remember best was tolerated punchball. You slapped the ball, a tennis ball, with your hand. Then you ran around the bases, first, second and home. It was more of a triangle than a diamond. But, you had to hit the ball over the outfielders' heads before you could even run to first. If an outfielder threw the ball home before you reached the base you were out. Nine innings of that!
I wasn't very good. But I was older so they tolerated me. I remember having a great time, even if it was *tolerated* punchball.

—*Jack Gilford*

Wiffle®Ball

Wiffle Ball is a relative newcomer to the world of Stickball. Mr. David Mullany of Fairfield, Connecticut, developed the Wiffle Ball during 1953-1954 when he found his son and a friend playing Yard Stickball with a plastic golfball. The game did not need a field, since only two players take part, and there was no base running involved. In addition, the light ball could not be thrown or hit far. The curious father asked his son what he called the game. "It's called Wiffle Ball," answered the son. The slang word "wiff" meant to "strike out" in Fairfield.

Since Mr. Mullany was a college and semi-pro baseball pitcher, he knew that trying to throw curves (see flukes -- Boxball) or sliders with a small light ball necessitates snapping the wrist or straining the arm. Eventually a young arm, wrist, or elbow could be damaged. To resolve this problem, the concerned father bought some plastic balls and cut holes in them with a razor. The design that worked best was a ball cut with holes on one side. This ball allowed curves to be thrown without snapping the wrist, it could be thrown straight, and when hit, traveled a shorter distance than a solid ball.

Mr. Mullany adopted the rules his son used in the backyard, and the Wiffle Ball was officially christened in 1955.

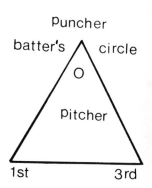

The Curve — The Wiffle Ball is thrown like a baseball and will curve very easily. The drawings below show how the ball should be held for curving and control.

OUT CURVE   **STRAIGHT**   **IN SHOOT**

To throw the ball straight — and this is important — the Wiffle Ball should be held as shown.

RULES:

(Adopted by permission of the Wiffle® Ball Co.)

The size of the playing field is optional, but we recommend a minimum dimension 20 feet (8 paces) by approximately 60 feet long (23 paces). The field is laid out with foul lines and markers for single, double, triple and home run areas. (See sketch of suggested playing field.)

The minimum number of players required to play Wiffle Ball are two — the pitcher and batter — one player to a side. The maximum number of players that can compete are ten — five players to a side. If a full team is playing, each side will consist of catcher, pitcher, double area fielder, and home run area fielders. Fielders cannot move from one area to another when a full team is playing. However, any number of players up to ten, can play Wiffle Ball. When more than two players are playing, captains for each side are picked and they choose their respective teams alternately. As in baseball the game is played with one team at bat and one team in the field. The batting order of the team at bat shall be Pitcher 1st., then following the Catcher, Double area player, Triple area player and home run area player. The rules of play are similar to baseball. Three outs to an inning retire a side, nine innings to a game. In case of tie, additional innings are played. For a complete inning both sides must bat. An out for the batter can be made in three ways:

1. The batter can strike out only if he swings at a pitched ball and does not foul tip the third strike. Foul tips count as a strike for the first two strikes. A foul tip caught in back of the batter's box does not count as an out.

2. Fly balls caught in fair or foul territory.

3. Ground balls caught while ball is in motion in fair territory. Bunting is not allowed. The batter cannot obtain a base on balls.

SCORING:

Single markers are placed approximately 24 feet from home plate on foul line. Ball hit in single area (i.e. area between batter's box and single markers) and not caught, constitutes a single. Double markers are placed approximately 20 feet in back of single markers on foul line. Ball hit in double area (area between single marker and double marker) and not caught, constitutes a double. Triple markers are placed on foul lines 20 feet back of double markers. Ball hit in triple area (area between double markers and triple markers) and not caught, constitutes a triple. Ball hit beyond the triple markers and not caught, constitutes a home run. The baseball rules of scoring runs apply. A player hits a single — his team has a man on first base (imaginary). The next player hits a single — his team now has an imaginary player on 1st. base and 2nd. base. The next player hits a home run — three runs score. The imaginary player on 1st. and 2nd. and the home run. A player advances one imaginary base on a single, 2 bases on a double and 3 imaginary bases on a triple. A player on 2nd. base scores on a single, double or triple. A player on 3rd. base scores on any hit.

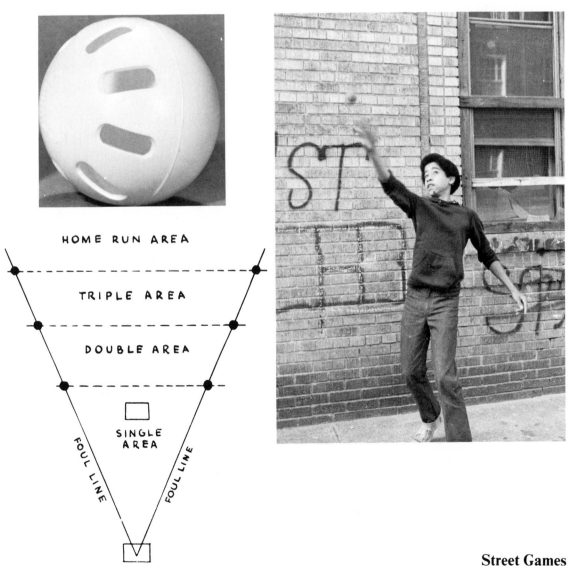

HOME RUN AREA

TRIPLE AREA

DOUBLE AREA

SINGLE
AREA

FOUL LINE

FOUL LINE

Chestnuts

ORIGIN:

The game of Chestnuts or Conkers, as they are called in England, did not even come into being until 150 years after the *Aesculus Hippocastanum,* or Chestnut Tree, was planted on the Island (England) in the beginning of the 17th century. There are records of a similar game played with Hazel Nuts, called Cobnuts (striking nuts) as early as the 15th century. Today, the game is played in several countries during the fall peaking by Thanksgiving.

EQUIPMENT:

1 16-inch lace (take it from a boot)
1 skewer
chestnuts (from a local tree, vendor or vegetable man)

TO MAKE THE WEAPON:

It is best to get a chestnut large enough to have strength but not so large as to be a vulnerable target. Hardness is checked by squeezing the end of the nut. If the shell is hard and feels solid through and through, it's a hard nut. This is ideal for the game.

Carefully put a skewer or nail through the center and lace it up, knotting the end.

The next step is to harden the nut. Baking it for half an hour or soaking it in salt and water, soda, or vinegar overnight are the favorite hardening procedures. An expert warrior suggested that all vinegar-soaked chestnuts be resoaked in water to get rid of the smell. Still another expert said the smell should be left in order to discourage others from getting too close to it. In either case, a player with a hard nut to crack is in good shape. War is but a step around the corner.

OBJECTIVE:

To destroy an opponent's chestnut and add years onto one's own (see scoring).

RULES:

First there is an encounter between two chestnut holders who go to battle. Whoever yells "first," or "firsties," goes first. There is a great advantage to going first, as in any first-strike attack. It is better to smash another's chestnut than have one's own smashed.

The "smashee" wraps the string around his finger, letting the chestnut hang ten to fourteen inches down. The nut must be stationary. While the nut rests, the smasher wraps his string several times around his two first fingers and proceeds to swing a shot at his opponent's chestnut from a distance of two or three feet. As long as the smasher continues to hit his target, he can keep shooting. The chestnut is brought to a standstill after each shot, since moving targets belong to another game. In the event the string becomes entwined during a shot, the first person to call "clinching" gets an extra shot. Once a shot is missed, the players reverse roles until one nut is totally obliterated and off the string.

SCORING:

There is a standard formula for calculating the age of a chestnut which has little to do with years (Carbon-14 is unnecessary). Any nut that has been lying in the closet for a year shrivels into a hard and deadly weapon called a "seasoner." Beware the seasoner -- scoring with a seasoner requires calculus.

A new chestnut that's never before been in battle winning over another makes the victor a one-yearer, or "one-er." Each victory adds years to the nut like any good war. If a one-er nut conquers a six-er, the victory compounds the age to a seven-er. The older (in victories) the nut is, the greater the challenge. By the end of autumn, the person with the oldest chestnut is champ. Most champs end a season with a fifty-er or sixty-er. If by some chance two old chestnuts should be crushed in a battle of the ages, then both scores are lost. There is no transferring accounts in this game.

WORLD RECORD
One of the all-time records was won in New England in a contest between a 362-er, 1,034-er, and 2,295-er. The winner of that match played a 3,559-er, and in the end, the tournament winner was a 7,453-er. For the sports nut, this is a great bag to get into.

Bottle Snatch or *Steal the Bacon*

ORIGIN:

The exact origin is unknown; however, in Indian folklore there are many references to a game with similar rules, using a block of wood or club.

OBJECTIVE:

To snatch the bottle from a point midway between two opposing sides and to carry the bottle (or can) back to the snatcher's side without being tagged. Takes very little mathematical, or even logical, know-how to make this geometric frolic a natural for passing the time.

Players are divided into two equal teams. Each team member has a number corresponding to one on the opposing side.

Everyone lines up along a designated starting base on the street or sidewalk. The starting base for each team is also the goal. The selected bottle (or can) is placed midway between the goals. Then the caller, the odd person or individual who enjoys exercising power, calls out one or more numbers. Once the number is called, the team players with that number run out from the base line and approach the bottle. (If two numbers are called, then four people will show up by the bottle, one person from each team for each number.)

When they reach the bottle or can, they circle, fake dodges, make false moves (even make obscene gestures) before snatching the bottle. Then the bottle is snatched by one, and the race is on. If the player makes it back to the starting base without being tagged by the opposite team's runner(s), he scores. There is no limit to how often a number can be called.

SCORING:

Each successful run is worth one point. The first team to reach eleven points (or whoever is ahead by dinner time) is the victor.

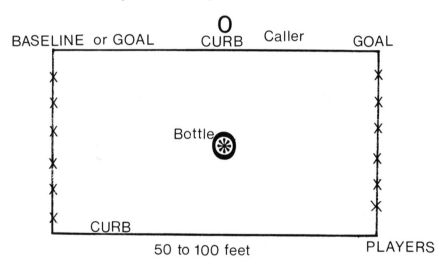

A goal or starting base line is marked off at one end of the street, and the second line, parallel and 50-100 feet from the starting base, is marked at the other end. The bottle or can is placed midway between the base lines and the two curbs.

Red Rover

ORIGIN:

Though this game is played in most countries around the world, it is difficult to pinpoint its birth. There is speculation that the game is an offshoot of the Scottish Jockey Rover, played full-swing by the late 1800's.

OBJECTIVE:

To dwindle the team chain of one side down to the point where only one man is left.

RULES:

Any number can play this exuberant game, which is associated with the rhyme:

Red rover, red rover,
Please send someone over.
Red rover, red rover,
Please send (Herbert, Tina, or Maxwell) over.

It is not associated with the delightful:

I'm looking over my dead dog Rover
That I overlooked before.
One leg is broken, the other is sprain.
He got run over by a cocoa-puff train.

But the results sometimes clearly come closer to the latter. The hazards of the game far outweigh the health benefits. Sprains, scrapes, and fractures are not uncommon, which seems to exercise no restraint on today's players. The danger is more of a catalyst in fact than a deterrent. Two teams face each other twenty feet apart on the lawn or curb of a street. Everyone grasps and locks hands, wrists, or elbows, forming a human chain. The team captain chants, "Red rover, red rover, please send someone over," naming one member of the opposite chain. The named person picks up steam and barrels into the chanting chain. (With a bit of luck, he will do better than poor dog Rover.)

In an effort to break the chain, the forward drive is accompanied with facial grimaces and wild animal screams. Force, with a touch of audio-visual effect, psychologically prepares (or destroys) the chain for the onslaught of the oncoming bulldozer.

It is also wise for the runner not to let on, until the very last moment, which member of the chain he is charging. The impact is more stunning and spectacular that way.

Should the runner fail to break the link of his choice, he becomes part of the chain. If he succeeds, he returns home with one member of the broken link. This is where the skill comes in. The captain must carefully weigh whom to call over--he wants someone who can become part of his team, but at the same time that risks having the chain broken and losing a member himself. Likewise, a runner can choose a weak or strong link. Surely, he can break a weak link and gain a weak player, but shooting for the strong links risks his being caught.

Even if the entire team collapses, as long as the chain remains intact, it can win the round. Each side takes alternate turns calling Rover, while the strength of a chain swings back and forth before a real winning pattern, or streak, emerges. The final aim is to reduce a team to one member before someone gets killed.

In some areas, the captains do not make the call. If there is an odd number of players, one person stands in the middle of the street and makes the calls for both teams.

VARIATIONS:
Red Rover sometimes varies, with all the players on top of a stoop or stairway. When called, they race down the steps into the human chain.

Red Lion

The one who is chosen "lion" lives on the sidewalk. All other players live in the middle of the road and frequent the curb, the border of the lion's den, while they are jeering:

> *Red lion, Red lion,*
> *Come out of your den.*
> *Whoever you catch*
> *Will be one of your men.*

When the "lion" senses the closeness of his tormentors, he leaps out to catch one of them. He must tag and say, "Red lion" three times to secure his game. Otherwise he is just a poacher. He and his prey return to the den to wait for the next round of tagging. Now the lion has one more person helping him hunt and capture victims from the jeering crowd. The final person left in the street (barring any sudden interference from trucks) wins. The safari ends, and both man and beast live happily ever after in the street.

Coins --
Flipping, Trading, Hitting, and Pitching

Guilderstern (flips a coin): The law of averages, if I have got this right, means that if six monkeys were thrown up in the air for long enough they would land on their tails about as often as they would land on their ....",

Rosencrantz and Guildenstern
by Tom Stoppard

ORIGIN:

Coins were first devised in Lydia and China. The earliest known sample is an electrum coin of Lydia, dating back to about 700 B.C. The first coins in America were issued by the Massachusetts Bay Company under the direction of John Hull in 1652. Other colonies followed the idea and the first United States mint was set up in 1792. But the first settlers had traded furs, shells, etc., for commodities, and the young colonists found it difficult to flip and pitch wampum and beaver furs.

The mint was located in Philadelphia, and by the year 1793, $50,000 in pennies and half-cents were in circulation. (The penny, an English import, was first introduced by Offa, King of Mercia, an old province of the Isles, which borrowed it from the Latin coin *denarri*, meaning pence.)

Today the games are found in all countries of the world, except Paraguay, the only coinless country. All penny games are popular from early spring through the summer and peak with the foliage.

Front and back of U.S.A. quarter honoring Bicentennial.

The little h Play.

PITCH *and* HUSSEL.

POISE your Hand fairly,
 And pitch plump your Slat;
Then fhake for all Heads,
 And turn down the Hat.

MORAL.

How fickle's this Game!
 So Fortune or Fate
Decrees our Repentance,
 When oft 'tis too late.

CRICKET.

From The Little Pretty Pocketbook published in 1744 by An Act of Parliament.

RULES:

Heads or Tails

One person flips the coin and while it's spinning in the air, he calls either heads or tails. If the flipper is not afraid of the penny going astray, he will let it hit the ground to determine the outcome. To add finesse to the game, however, the player can stop and catch the descending coin in the palm of his hand and slap it over onto his wrist, in effect, giving the coin one more turn before eyeing the answer. If the caller has guessed the outcome correctly, he wins and keeps the cash. The loser supplies the next coin and assumes the role of flipper. Both players are subservient to the laws of chance (and those of supply and demand).

Penny Pitching

In this form of off-track betting, all the gamblers line up along the curb and throw their pennies to the wall (for the majority, also to the wind). The pitcher who gets his penny closest to the wall scoops up all the cash.

One variation, popular in the inner city, is to play the penny on the rebound -- that is, the penny closest to the wall after it hits the wall wins the match. If a penny fails to hit the wall, it's an automatic loss, or "zilch." There is always one steady winner on the block who doesn't hesitate to jangle his overweight pockets in superior glee or make friends through lending schemes.

1787--Indian copper.
$2,500.

Hit the Penny

EQUIPMENT:

   a spaldeen or handball
   1 penny
   1 sidewalk

RULES:

Two players stand on the sidewalk approximately two sidewalk boxes, or eight feet, apart. Each player stands behind the line or crack in the cement of his box. The common crack between the boxes is the center line upon which the penny is placed. The object is to hit the penny to gain points. It is important that each player hit the penny carefully so as not to move or push the penny closer to his opponent. (It is obviously easier to hit a coin that is closer.) Additionally, a player trying to regain his coin position will find it more and more difficult, because the angle at which the ball hits the coin only continues to move it further away.

1787--George Clinton
Copper $2,500.

SCORING:

If the penny is hit by the ball and doesn't move, the shot is worth one point. If the penny flips over once on the shot, it's five points. Whoever earns twenty-one points is the winner. Marathon games are usually limited to 100 points.

Whoever coined the phrase, "a penny saved is a penny earned," played the game and scored his point.

1787 Indian, N.Y. Arms
$2,300.

1785--Constellatio
$1500.

Pussy Wants a Corner or Puss-Puss

ORIGIN:

The game has been documented as early as the 17th century in Sweden, Italy, and England. (In Russia, the puss was an ox and was played quite frequently before the Bolsheviks did their thing.) The game is found all over the world today, where only the name of the animal seems to vary rather than the rules.

OBJECTIVE:

The idea is to tantalize the Pussy without letting it get into one's own spot or corner.

RULES:

The game must be played with five people. Four of the five players find a corner to stand in, and the fifth lonely player is the Pussy.

The Pussy stands erect in the center, equidistant from each corner. The type of corner used -- drawn bases, manhole covers, street lights, or parking signs -- often determines the shape of the playing field. The game itself is very much like stealing bases in baseball, except that the corner players try to exchange (steal) bases or places with one another. In effect, the Pussy is the ball which tries to beat the runner out to a base. More specifically, the corner players confer simplistically with Pussy, shouting, ''Puss-Puss, come to my corner.''

Just when the dialogue heats up, the corner players reply, ''Go to my next-door neighbor.'' In a similar vein, the gamesters lure Pussy in one direction, with little intention of following through with any action. In fact, a player tries to put Pussy on a course diametrically opposed to the direction in which the player plans to move. Red herrings!

When two players think Pussy is preoccupied with one corner, they dash diagonally across the playing area or to the nearest corner if they're smart. If the Pussy gets to one of the vacant corners while they play switchies, the runner without a corner is the next Pussy. Tactically, the clever Pussy pretends to look or plead in one direction while actually tempting the corners behind its back to switch places. The runners are unaware of the Pussy's sneakiness, and bang--one of them is caught. Once the running begins, any number of corner players can exchange places, while Pussy frantically races around in search of an empty corner. Once everyone abandons his ''place in the sun,'' confusion sets in, tactics cease, someone miscalculates and ends up without a corner. Alas, the next Pussy is thus born. For the new Pussy, it is a bit like baseball's force play. He was on first and ran to second on the next hit, only to discover the man on second hadn't moved. There is an exchange of forbidding glances, a sigh of uh-oh, and he is out!

Hydrants

ORIGIN:

The fire hydrant evolved from the "fire plug" used in early wooden water systems. Metal hydrants appeared in Hamburg, Germany, at the end of the 18th century.

The first hydrant to be installed in the United States was of the wooden type, in Philadelphia, in 1801. Within ten years, Philly had over 400 hydrants. Today, there are over 3,000,000 units, with New York as leader of the pack with 140,000 hydrants. Unlike hub caps, these summer fountains remain intact over the years. Though hydrants are about 300 times the value of a hub, they weigh, on the average, 750 pounds, which makes theft or trading a bit cumbersome. (Frederick Graff, of the Philadelphia Waterworks, has been declared the "Father of the American Hydrant.")

OBJECTIVE:

To pass the time and cool off on hot summer days.

EQUIPMENT:

1 monkey wrench
Tin cans or garbage pail covers

RULES:

This game flourishes when the humidity and heat are high. Once a wrench is found, someone with strength must take off the side cap and open the valve -- usually an older brother or sister, who exchanges such service for an oral promise of eternal love (or "covering" for them in the future). When the water is running, any of several games is played, each with the ultimate purpose of soaking everyone and everything on the block.

Shoot the Can

The first of these joys is to place an empty tin can over the spurting hydrant, let go--and watch the thrust of the water "shoot your can off." The can that flies the highest earns the proud owner the title "King Can." Measuring methods are still primitive, but most people support the judgment of the strongest kid on the block.

It should be noted that the path of the descent of a can, once fired off, is of little concern for the players, though for pedestrians it provides a challenge.

★ *War* ★

This is a highly disorganized game played with tin cans (both ends cut out) or garbage pail covers. Pressing the can or covers against the spray, the water direction can be skillfully manipulated. (It's very much like shaking a bottle of coke with your thumb over the top.) If there are adjacent hydrants, war can be declared between them. More often, however, it's one man -- the General -- against a host of running victims who hide behind cars across the street. Those brave souls who enjoy water, courageously dash across, reaching the hydrant dripping wet in an effort to turn the tide and soak the General. Then "peace with wetness" is declared until a new General takes over the hydrant. All innocent passers-by observe this frolic and shift to the other side of the street, creep under a car, or turn back and walk down another block.

Finally, there is the unspoken war between the motorist and the water children. This game, making any passing car a great target for hydrant gunners, is a misconstrued version of "In and Out the Window." Suspecting attack, the hydrophobic driver defends himself by frantically reaching over the seat, rolling up the windows, while driving with the other hand. But for the trusting motorist, who thinks to himself, "How cute the kids look running through the sprinkler," disaster is but a moment away. The gunners grin with delight, anticipating the splashing anger from their sitting duck. As the car drives by, the command, "Fire!" is given, and a soaked, shaken driver slams on his brakes. In an angry daze, with little frolic left in his heart, he is seen making an unsubtle hand gesture at his foes, who have taken cover behind a car or in the house. The warriors watch the car slowly pull away and await their next car-wash victim.

Johnny on the Pony or Buck-Buck

Roman d'Alexandre, 14th century.

ORIGIN:

Johnny on the Pony is a variation on the theme Leapfrog, most probably a derivative of Buck-Buck. *"Bucca Bucca quot sunt hic?"* (Buck Buck how many are these?) was questioned in the time of Nero. There is documentation that it was played in Italy, England, and Turkey in the 17th century. Later it was imported here from England, where there are over fifty names for the game today. Questioning "how many fingers" has been deleted from the game. Ethnic makeup of a community tends to determine nomenclature and the game becomes "Moshe or Tony on the Pony."

OBJECTIVE:

This exercise of strength and stamina demonstrates team brawn superiority. The mere fact that one plays the game raises serious questions about the brains.

RULES:

First, the group is divided into two teams. Generally, captains pick the strongest and heaviest kids.

After the teams are divided, one team transforms itself into a pony. One thin member of the team is designated the pillow or cushion. He stands with his back against a wall or lamppost, allowing the second member of the team to nuzzle his head in the pillow's stomach. It is the pillow's job to absorb the impact of the opposing team leaping on the pony.

When the first person wraps his arms around the waist of the pillow, he spreads his legs two or three feet apart. The next player, with his head to the side or between the preceding player's legs, secures his arms around the preceding player's thighs.

The process continues until all team members are interlocked. Weaker or smaller teammates are relegated to the extremities of the pony, leaving the strength to the middle.

Now the pony is ready to ride, and the pillow yells out a signal like, "Go!", "Ride 'em" (big in the midwest), or "Here comes" or "God have mercy on our unique anatomical features" (big in New York). The game is set in motion and whoever goes first, leaps as far as he can onto the pony, making room for those who follow. Each rider lands on the pony as hard as he can in an effort to bust it.

Once landed, he straddles the pony, holding on for dear life. He is not allowed to move forward. If a rider's feet (any part) touch the ground, or if the rider falls off, the round is forfeited for the entire team. Then team spirit and body proceed to crush him.

The ultimate strategy for the riders is to land on the weakest link on the pony and hope for collapse. The increasing weight over a period of time can surely do a pony in. The pillow shouts, "Hurry! Come on!" while the other team captain is buying ice cream for his team or casually asking for the next runner ("Where's Willy?"). Once all the riders have jumped aboard, and the pony remains intact, the pillow calls out, often gasping:

> *Johnny on the pony 1-2-3*
> *Johnny on the pony 1-2-3*
> *Johnny on the pony 1-2-3*
> *All off.*

During those last moments, the riders intensify their effort to bust the pony, while the pony moves and bounces to shake, or finally knock, the riders off balance. The one thing a pony member can never do is pick up his head. "Heads" is not a legal way to get rid of your opponent, but it's a sure way to give him a hernia.

Should the pony and the riders collapse simultaneously, the team that hits the dirt with cries of, "Don't step on my lips!" loses. If the pony is still a pony at the end of the pillow's call, the pony wins. Then the pony team members become the jumpers and the jumpers become the pony. The team with the fewest fractures, greater number of winning rounds, or the team which is just able to walk at the end of the day, wins.

"Buck-buck, how many fingers have I got up?"

Mother May I or Giant Steps ?

ORIGIN:

This game is known as "Mother May I?," or "Giant Steps," and was played in England at the turn of the 19th century. Though the exact beginning is unclear, there are many early games that bear strong resemblance. Most definitive of these is "Judge and Jury," founded in despotism, tyranny, and total disregard of English law. But the game has grown in popularity all over the world, particularly in Australia, Yugoslavia, and the United States. In Israel, it is called *Aba,* meaning father. However, even in Germany, the only country which refers to itself as the Fatherland, it is still called, "Mother May I?"

OBJECTIVE:

Uniquely, the game appears to lack any logical objective, though it remains a joyous and popular choice among kids. In this seemingly irrational game, all the power is left to the caller, who doesn't hesitate to show his likes and dislikes of the players during the game. There's not a semblance of fairness, no matter how closely it resembles the old game Judge and Jury.

The practical objective of the game is to get across the street toward the caller, who, while setting the pace, waits as the players move closer and closer. If the caller wants to keep his post, he is sure to make this a lengthy business.

RULES:

The game is enjoyed mostly by girls in England, but in the United States, both sexes revel in it. One person is chosen leader or caller. Whoever says "leader" first, is usually the one who's up. The rest of the players then line up along the curb on the side of the street opposite the caller. When there is a rare sense of fairness, the leader keeps his back to the others who are designated by numbers or names other than their own. The usual, however, is for the caller to face the enemy and favor the players he likes.

The caller tells one subject he may approach him, taking some unusual or peculiar step. Before taking the step, the player must question: "Mother May I?" (or just "May I?"). If the subject fails to ask the question properly before he moves, he is required to return to the starting line.

The dialogue, answering a statement with a question, goes something like this:

> *Caller: Irving, you may take three baby steps.*
> *Irving: May I?*
> *Caller: You may.*

At which Irving takes three steps forward. However, the caller can change his mind and answer:

> *Caller: No you may not; you may take three giant steps.*
>   *(Or: You may take no steps at all.)*
> *Irving: May I?*

And so on. The mad dialogue continues for every player, every step of the way. The emphasis is not on winning but on the genuine joy derived from watching a friend looking assinine. It's a marathon race with the Mad Hatter.

BASIC STEPS:
   Baby Step -- A small step the length of a shoe.
   Giant Step-- As long as one can step from a standing position.
   Running Giant Step -- Same as above, but with a running start.
   Curb and Back -- Player must run back to the starting line and run forward until the caller tells him to stop.
   Backward Step -- One step backward.
   Wooden Soldier Step -- One step forward, the body in a stiff position.

Goose Step -- A soldier step, kicking one leg forward at a time without bending the knees.

Umbrella Step -- Putting one's arm up, pointing the forefinger into the top of the head, while spinning around forward (all at the same time).

Scissor Step -- A jump forward with both feet apart and a second jump with the feet together on the landing.

Banana Step -- Starting in a standing position, one leg is slipped forward as far as possible, and the rear leg is brought up after in each stride.

Twirling Step -- Twirling around on one foot with both arms pointed straight out.

Seal Step -- Hands face out from the body to touch palms down to the ground, while the feet drag behind like a seal.

Inchworm -- Inching up, lying on the stomach, face into the ground, groveling in the dirt, butt up. (Biting the dust is most accurate.)

Any combination of these steps, or a particular step, and the quantity the player may take are all within the province of the caller.

VARIATION:

In some areas the street crossers name the type of step they wish to take. For example:

> *Irving: May I take two Scissor Steps?*
> *Caller: You may (or: You may not) or he simply changes the request.*
> *Irving: May I? (whether or not the wish is granted).*

If a player should get close to the caller and tag him, the caller chases his challenger back to the starting line. If he tags the challenger before reaching the line, he still remains the caller. But if he fails, the player who has been subservient to the caller, usurps his power. The new caller continues in the same spirit. But the plan of action followed by most callers is to prolong the game until everyone wants to quit rather than make the tag.

Mother, May I take two Baby Steps?

Flies Up, Kick Ball, and Tip Cat

ORIGIN:

When it was a hot day, and too few players showed up for a ball game, an adaptation of Stickball, Punchball, and Slapball came about. It is like Punch- or Slapball in that the ball is not pitched to the batter. It's a batter do-it-yourself job called "fungo." Hitting fungo has been popular in heavily populated cities since 1910, and Tip Cat, a game of hitting a stick, peaked in popularity in the late '20's-early '30's.

EQUIPMENT:

rubber kickball or spaldeen
bat or stick
piece of whittled wood, one end carved to a point (tip-cat)

OBJECTIVE:

Unlike Baseball, there are no plays in this game. All balls are hit fungo simply in an effort to get the ball past a fielder.

RULES:

Flies Up

The batter tosses the ball in the air and slams a grounder or fly. Even if the fielder makes the catch, he must perform successfully the following arduous task before replacing the batter. First, the batter places the bat or stick on the ground in a position perpendicular to himself. Second, the fielder rolls the ball at the stick from where he caught it. If the ball misses the stick, the throw and catch were worthless efforts. Even if the ball hits the stick, the batter can save his reign if he catches the ball off the bat on a fly. If he misses, he is immediately replaced by the fielder.

Kickball

The ball is kicked fungo and the after-catch ritual of hitting the stick is eliminated. Instead, the batter is allowed as many kicks as he wants until the fielder has caught three flies and four grounders. The only way to stay kicking is to get the ball past the opposition. The kicker isn't penalized for any ball missed by a fielder.

WHO WILL BELL THE CAT?

Tip Cat

In the West it is called Hit (or Slam) the Stick; in the Midwest, Tippy; and in the East, Pussy. It has been a street staple since it arrived from the shores of England during the early Colonial days.

A stick about six inches long and two inches thick is carved into a "cat." One end is carved to a point, so that the pointed side is a wedge. The stick is placed on the ground so that there is a space between the carved end and the pavement. The batter slams the cat, sending it straight up in the air before him. With lightning speed, he madly swings the broomstick bat, sending the descending cat into the field before it hits the ground again. If the man up misses the cat three times or if it is caught on a fly, he is out. Fielding is unlikely -- it takes courage to field a pointed stick.

Tipping the cat does not count as a strike or miss against the batter.

For slight variation, the players form a line and each takes a turn at hitting the cat. Each shot is marked off in the street. Whoever hits it furthest, wins.

Statues

ORIGIN:

Statues, in its simplest form, was evidenced in the 19th century on the country roads of Europe. Over the past hundred years, the game has been amended with so many complications and dimensions that much of the original game has been lost. In America, the game is so much a standard that for generations throughout the country it has been a reminder of a common heritage in a common childhood.

OBJECTIVE:

To propel friends through the air, converting them into works of art upon landing.

RULES:

Any number of people can play this baffling game. A group of eight- or nine-year-olds lines up against the curb, a car, or tree and waits to be pulled by the arm into the middle of the road or yard. One player -- designated "puller", "twister", or "yanker"--walks up to each waiting soul and asks, "Do you want coffee, tea, or milk?"

> *coffee -- a gentle pull*
> *tea -- a firm tug*
> *milk -- a generous yank*

There are variations to the lingo: "bread, water, or honey," "sugar, salt, or pepper," "heaven, limbo, hell," etc. Whatever the nomenclature, the player at least has a chance to suggest the desired thrust of propulsion. His reply is only a suggestion, though, and the results often reflect the whimsy of the twister or his relationship to the person being yanked. The anticipation of how rough, or how far, one's flight will be is the root of the game's excitement. After a player is propelled forward, he is expected to freeze like a stone "statue," in whatever position he falls on landing.

In some rural areas, the method of sending off a human projectile differs. In one popular variety, the twister spins each player by the arms, in a circle, before letting go at random. If the arm sockets remain intact, he is halfway there. At least he's had a safe take-off.

A safe landing is another story. One broken statue, and the game is over for at least a week.

Providing blast-off and recovery are successful, the statue commonly remains in an awkward, motionless, stoned position or risks being ousted from the game. All portions of the statue, including facial expressions, must remain frozen until signaled otherwise by the twister. When all the players have been blasted (off), the twister views his museum of statuary. With bizarre aesthetic taste, the twister taps those statues with the least artistic appeal, releasing them from bondage. All the statues must keep their eyes shut until tapped.

At long last, there remains a statue -- an artistic hallmark of mankind -- the most distorted, contorted, ugliest, grimaced, and pained individual left standing with his eyes shut to a circle of admirers. The museum goers' "oo's" and "ah's" are replaced by giggles, snickers, and whispers. If the final statue doesn't burst into tears, the puller signals to the group that it's time for a song. Through the streets of the gallery, the chorus chants in unison:

Wake up sleeping beauty,
You're the one.
Wake up, sleepy head,
Wake up! wake up!

(or something along those lines). This final statue hears the magic song, sees the light, and becomes the next twister.

VARIATIONS:

All the statues are allowed to keep their eyes open after they land. Once everyone has been yanked or pulled, the twister commands each player to act out in pantomime a different animal or object. The twister judges the performances, much to the amusement of the other players. The funniest or cleverest, by the standards of eight-year-olds, is the winner.

Deadest

This cheery variation called "Playing Dead" or "Deadest," is for those fascinated with the rituals of the hereafter. After being thrown by the twister, each player must die in the position in which he lands. As in all the action-packed westerns and war movies, the fallen victim dramatically writhes in pain, contorts his body, shouts, groans before hitting the pavement. Lacking empathy, the twister may even go for a lunch break before judging the murders of the 'Rue Morgue.' Hopefully, he returns to judge before a car does. The one who is the stillest and most convincing corpse wins -- ghoulish, foolish, and fun.

statues
because you get to be a
stachue and you can twirl
the people and pick who's the
best one
Lori Kirschner

Age 7

New York

Kick the Can

ORIGIN:

Even before the awareness of noise pollution, Kick the Can was irritating neighbors as early as the mid-19th century in England. The game was probably played earlier in quieter fashion with wood blocks or sticks. With the emergence of the tin can, however, noise became vital in the enjoyment of the game. How much *fun* could it be if it didn't annoy the neighborhood? In Britain, it is most commonly referred to as "Tin Can Tommy" by the younger population. (The adults call it something else.)

EQUIPMENT:

3 or more humans
1 tin can

OBJECTIVE:

To keep the chosen seeker, or "it," from capturing his playmates while they try to release those already caught -- in effect, keeping "it" on the run.

RULES:

Once a tin can is found in the backyard, alley way, or garbage pail, one person is designated "it," or seeker, which is quite undesirable in this game. The selection is made by picking numbers or by the "not it" method (see Choosing Sides), though the most common procedure is: everyone goes out searching for a can and the last one back is the seeker. The only drawback is that once a player realizes he's been searching too long for his can, he may head for home rather than be "it." Sometimes no one comes back at all.

Kick the can

It is a game played by groups of people as many as you want but it has to be an even team. Say there are three teams of two and one guy is it. Then one guy kicks the can a far as he can to. Then after 60 seconds the guy who is it picks it up and put it back in its original place. Then the other guys go hide. The the two who is it starts crossing and when they catch one he is a prisoner. Then when a guy comes and kicks the can then the prisoner is free. The game ends when everybody is caught.

MARK   Age 13

The seeker draws a circle on the street or finds a sewer cover to be the can's tabernacle. With reverence, the tin can is placed on the altar. Moments later, any player other than the seeker kicks the can out of this place of worship, trumpeting all to run and hide while the seeker retrieves the can.

In some neighborhoods, the seeker, before he retrieves the can, must count to one hundred and walk around the sewer several times -- depending on how much the group dislikes "it."

In either case, the can must be retrieved and replaced on the altar before "it" can go on his search for other players. Once the seeker spots someone, he must run back to his canned house of worship, bang the can, and call out the sighted friend's name with the benediction, "Kick the can, one, two, three." The named person must answer the call and come out of hiding to stand by the can.

Any hiding player within hearing distance is aware that a comrade has been caught. When the seeker resumes his search, any player can come to the rescue of a captured friend. In order to break through any security precautions set up by the seeker, the rescuer must be unobserved by "it" so that he can kick the can out again. This is the only way to free a prisoner.

Once the seeker hears his can go off, he knows what's happened. Until the can is back on the altar, circle, or sewer, he is powerless to call or capture anyone. He is also faced with the double problem of leaving the can to find hiders while having to run back to check that prisoners aren't released. This conflict builds frustration and anxiety in "it." The only relief is to vary the game so that after a person has been caught a certain number of times, he then becomes the new and conflict-ridden "it."

The noise of the can, irate neighbors, and the running around in circles, can make this a game of joy or misery, depending on how one gets his kicks.

I know many people are familiar with all the versions of "Hide and Seek" and "Kick the Can", but I wonder if anyone of my generation recalls, "Fox in the Morning": One lone person would stand on one side of the street, arraigned against how many players were available at the time. The single player was 'the fox', the many players were 'the geese'. The fox would yell across the street, "Fox in the morning", the multiple players would retort, "Geese in the evening". The fox would yell, "How many are there?" The geese would reply, "More than you can catch!!" That would be the signal for all to take off, the idea being for the geese to reach the opposite curb without the fox tagging anyone of them. If the fox tagged any one of the geese, they would come over to his side, until the game dwindled down to everyone being caught.

This was one of my favorite games in my earlier years because I was truly an artful dodger, and probably reached my greatest heights of success participating in this particular sport, until at the age of ten, baseball and football took me completely over.

Best regards,

Gene Kelly

Running Bases

ORIGIN:

There is no question that running bases is a bastardized version of Baseball, adapted to the street field. It is a wholly American game, born on the streets of New York in the late 1800's. Across the country, it is known by such names as Taggin' Up, Fag Tag, and Bag Ball.

Rules

The way you play running base is is that you have 2 cheaters opposite each other. Then the other people get on base. Everybody runs to a base when they throw the ball back and forth. If a person gets tagged with the ball it become one of the cheaters or catchers.

Ⓒ Doreen
Age 9
Omaha, Nebraska

EQUIPMENT:

at least three players
1 rubber or tennis ball

RULES:

Two spots on the street are designated bases -- usually chalk circles about sixty feet apart or two sewers when convenient. The area between the bases and the curbs is running territory. Two players, each standing on one of the bases, have a catch with the ball. The players who are having the catch slowly move in on the runners who try to outmaneuver the catchers and reach a base safely.

If a runner dodges, outruns, or bypasses a baseman who no longer has the ball (and reaches the base), the baseman relinquishes his job to the runner (only in a game with three people). Whenever a baseman has the ball, he can tag the runner, putting him out of the game as in Baseball (when there are more than three players). The ball cannot be thrown at a player for a tag (only for inflicting a black eye or a bump on the head). The slap of a spaldeen is a real stinger. In essence, the game is the forced play found in Baseball. A runner caught between first and second or second and third tries to outfox the baseman, who tosses the ball to and fro. The runner vigorously shimmies between the oncoming baseman, who tries to run him down, and the position of the ball in the air. The runner's best bet is to get past a baseman just as he throws it to the other man. More often, the runner just speeds back and forth till he's a cornered rat and is tagged out. When there is more than one runner, the advantages run in the runners' favor.

Compared with Baseball, Running Bases is the more hazardous game. In

Baseball, rarely does one see a car bulleting down the base line. The only street precaution taken is a general alarm sounded by one of the eagle-eyed.

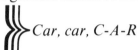
Car, car, C-A-R

This is the only time the game halts, providing everyone gets out of the way of the oncoming car. Very often players are confident that a car won't hit them, and the car driver is convinced that a kid isn't stupid enough to stay in his way.

Once a car has passed, and there are as many players as there were before the interruption, the game resumes. In addition to the danger of cars, sliding into the base tends to be more bodily degrading on asphalt than on astro-turf. If one must slide, it is better to slide in on shoes than sneakers or crepe soles. Sliding on rubber shifts the forward momentum into a head-first landing.

WORLD RECORDS FOR STEALING BASES	
Most Bases Stolen in One Game	7—George F. Gore (Chicago), June, 1881.
	William Hamilton (Phila.), August, 1894.
Most Bases Stolen in One Season (Since 1900)	118—Lou Brock (St. Louis), 1974.
Most Bases Stolen in Lifetime	937—William Hamilton (Phila.), 1888–1901.

Simon Says

ORIGIN:

The date of origin is unknown, though there are references to a game called Wiggle-Waggle as early as 1850. In this game, the leader either turned his thumbs up or down, and the group would have to follow suit instantaneously. Anyone who responded slowly or incorrectly was out of the game. The old thumbing gesture rings strongly of the arena games of ancient Rome. Far removed from the Colosseum, it has been reported that the modern-day version of Do This, Do That was unveiled officially in the Borscht Belt of New York's Catskill Mountains, when a social director named Simon, in one of the hotels, converted Do This, Do That to Simon Says, and the game quickly swept the countryside.

OBJECTIVE:

In this game of elimination, the players, in order to stay in the game, must imitate the leader quickly and correctly on certain commands.

RULES:

The version played today is a hybrid of earlier traditions. One person is elected leader, and the rest of the group stand in front of him to perform their acts of submission. He starts the mimicry with the famous phrase, "Simon says," and then a command: "Jump up, sit down, roll over, clap hands," etc. The entire group must obey immediately. Anyone failing to perform efficiently is exiled from the "pleasure dome."

In an effort to create confusion, the leader fires orders in rapid succession. Then he calls off a command without preceding it with "Simon says ..." Anyone executing such an unauthorized order is eliminated. Tricky!

The type of feat, the rapidity of the orders, and the frequency of the quick switch in the orders lies solely at the discretion of the leader. Most leaders, inflated with power, are rarely discreet. The last player left (aside from Simon) wins the game and accedes to the Simonian throne in the next game.

VARIATION:

The variation is actually the predecessor of Simon Says and is played in the same manner except for the delivery of the commands. The command "Do this" is the command to follow, whether or not it is preceded by "Simon says ...". All commands of "Do that" are *nicht*. If the players are doing jumping jacks and the leader changes to clapping hands, for example, everyone should continue with the jumping jacks until the new stunt is preceded with the appropriate "Do this." Any player doing what the leader does on "that" instead of "this" is out of the game.

Sometimes commands are delivered so fast that one's own reflexes do him in. The exceptional and scientific Simon (Legree) makes ridiculous orders: "Jump up," without including "Come down," which lands an argument early in the game. It's a great game when everyone on the block shows up and there is only one spaldeen on hand.

Flinch

ORIGIN:

No one person has been credited with this witless pastime, though it is one of the few surviving traditions from barbarian tribes.

OBJECT:

To test reflexes by the use of anticipatory pain.

RULES:

Two players face each other, standing a foot apart. One player holds his hands behind his back while the other places them directly out in front of him at the height of his abdomen. The latter player's palms should face each other, in the position of praying hands. And he has good reason to pray -- for within a moment, the attacker will shift his shoulder to forewarn of the oncoming swat of his hand. However, it may be only a false alarm or fake out, not followed through with the hand. If the victim, during a false alarm, moves his hands, or "flinches," the attacker is entitled to take a free shot. He is permitted (or allowed) to hit the victim full force for each "flinch." The only defense the imperiled player has is to move his hands out of the way of a real attack.

If the attacker misses, the roles reverse. This is the game's only saving grace. But should he land a good blow, a stinging pain precedes a loud expression of distress.

Avoiding the real McCoy explains the reflex action or "flinch," but understanding that does not change the outcome of the game. There are several positions and techniques to vary the game's format, but the pain-principle remains throughout them all. One person extends his hands, palms facing the ground, and the attacker in this case meets his victim's palms with his own. The attacker flicks his wrist slightly or bounces his opponent's hand to cause him to flinch. If the scared recipient of such good will moves his hands away, the aggressor gets one free shot. The attacker can also make a wide arc and slap his opponent's left hand with his own left hand or, more safely, the one closest directly above his palm. One miss and the position of hands changes.

Another variation is for two players to stand facing each other, arms extending up and outward. The thrust is for one player either to push over his opponent or fake him into making a forward attack. A forward attack, met with no resistance, tends to send the attacker face forward onto the pavement. The first player to lose his balance loses.

Though it is rare in this country and popular in England, there is one game in which the target is one player's head, while the attacker holds his handy weaponry behind his back. The victim is supposed to duck in case of a real attack. However, should contact be made with the pair of swinging hands, there will be little reason to change roles. Whatever the motion or means of attack, the name of the game stays the same--pain. (See Glossary-''Slapsies'')

Picture next page: If not picked for the hockey team, you're dressed for ''Slapsies.''

POM-POM PULL-AWAY

ORIGIN:

In England the game is more commonly called Wall-to-Wall and has been played since the early 1700's. The game traveled to the United States from England in the 20th century. Pom-Pom Pull Away is popular in most urban areas but has a stronger rooting in Maine and Minnesota where the street version is converted into an ice-skating spectacle. After the northern lakes thaw, Pull Away is resumed in the streets.

OBJECTIVE:

The person who is "it" tries to tag people crossing the street so that "it" gains all the players who were running against him. (High-level politics!)

RULES:

This city street game is most exciting with fifteen or more players. Any running between the curbs is fair but dangerous territory. The sidewalks is the only safe area for a runner. "It" must stand in the middle of the street while all the other players line up along one side of the curb. "It" calls out a friend's name with the following chant:

Pom-pom pull away,
If you don't come,
I'll fetch you away.

The named player runs across the street toward the opposite curb, while "it" tries to tag him before reaching the other side. (There is a strong resemblance to a Red Rover variation.)

Once the runner makes it safely to the sidewalk, he remains there until all the other players have been called. Anyone caught by "it" stays in the middle of the road to help tag the remaining players. Eventually, there will be more people in the middle, with the power of "it," than on the curb. No matter how many are caught in the middle, only "it" calls out names. The players running from curb to curb find their plight more and more difficult with each succeeding turn. The last runner is the winner.

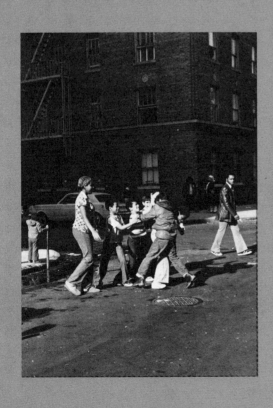

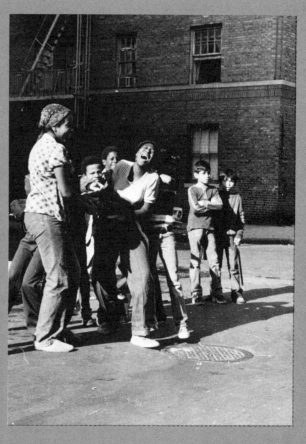

The Safety Patrol System emulates the organization of the police force with patrolmen, sergeants, lieutenants, and captains. Upon appointment by the sixth-grade teacher, each recruit is given a white shoulder belt and silver badge as symbol of his authority. The system is clean cut and reports little corruption from within (despite the report that one individual was busted for selling firecrackers while on duty).

However, as with all organizations, even the Safety Patrol has come in for its share of problems. An election was held in a city junior high school, where the safety program was carried on through the elective process rather than by teacher appointment. In fact, the eighth grade of this particular school was modeled after the average municipal structure (which is probably where the trouble started).

In this case, a nominee for Safety Commissioner approached his opponent with the offer, "I'm unbeatable, but I'll help you out." His convincing argument was, "You can't win, and if you don't campaign, I'll appoint you as my Deputy Commissioner when I'm elected. If you do campaign, you'll lose anyway, and you end up with nothing. So you might as well not campaign!"

His opponent agreed, and the wheeler-dealer won the election.

At the end of the year came graduation, and the elected official was given the Sportsmanship Award for being the first Safety Commissioner to appoint his opponent as his Deputy.

On the brighter side, it must be noted that many safety patrolmen have been awarded medals for outstanding performance and for saving lives.

THE LAW Playing in the street is hazardous and therefore an area of concern to law enforcement agencies (rather than a legal battlefield). There are general laws covering Disorderly Conduct, Health and Safety, Obstruction of Traffic, Inciting a Riot, etc., which apply to gamesters even though actual prosecution is unlikely. The laws, in fact, are often so general and abstrusely framed as to be applicable to everyone. For example, in Oklahoma, nuisance is defined as one who:

First. Annoys, injures or endangers the comfort, repose, health, or safety of others; or,

Second. Offends decency; or,

Third. Unlawfully interferes with, obstructs or tends to obstruct, or renders dangerous for passage, any lake or navigable river, stream, canal or basin, or any public park, square, street or highway; or,

Fourth. In any way renders other persons insecure in life, or in the use of property. R.L. 1910 4250.

The laws covering the Public Peace are more specific, while covering a wider range of behavior. In Los Angeles County, for one, the crimes and corresponding punishments range from $10.00 to 20 years imprisonment:

647. Disorderly conduct

Who loiters in or about any toilet open to the public for the purpose of engaging in or soliciting any lewd or lascivious or any unlawful act.

415. Disturbing the peace; noise; use of public streets of unincorporated town for offensive conduct, horse racing, or shooting; indecent language; punishment

Any person or persons holding, or conducting, or participating in, or using any vulgar, profane, or indecent language within the presence or hearing of women or children, in a loud and boisterous manner, is guilty of a misdemeanor, and upon conviction by any Court of competent jurisdiction, shall be punished by fine not exceeding two hundred dollars, or by imprisonment in the County Jail for not more than ninety days, or by both fine and imprisonment, or either, at the discretion of the Court.

In Detroit, Michigan, the issue of public versus private playing is in the forefront.

Sec. 58-1-9 of the Detroit City Code, codifying the 1954 compiled Ordinances (Chap. 330), 11 (a), provides:

"No person shall play any game of nine or ten pins, ball, cricket or other games in any street, alley, or other public place."

Pedestrian safety rather than gamester safety seems to be the overriding concern of most legislators. In Albuquerque, New Mexico, the "discharging of weapons in the city and the propulsion of missles towards homes and people" is strictly prohibited. This, however, does not necessarily apply to stickball, basketball or football, unless the broken window belongs to the mayor.

Salt Lake City, Utah, left little to the imagination when drawing up its statutes. Again, the main concerns are pedestrian safety or peace and obstruction of traffic. The laws listed below are still in effect, though enforcement might prove difficult, if not impossible.

"(Cities or towns) may prohibit or regulate the rolling of hoops, playing of balls, flying of kites, riding of bicycles or tricycles, or any other amusements or

Auto Club Distinguished Service Medal being given to Safety Patrol Heroes.

practices having a tendency to annoy persons passing in the streets or on sidewalks, or to frighten teams of horses, or to interfere with traffic." Utah Code Annotated 10-8-69.

"(Cities or towns) may prevent the ringing of bells, blowing of horns and bugles, crying of goods by auctioneers and others, and the making of other noises, for the purpose of business, amusement or otherwise, and prevent all performances and devices tending to the collection of persons on the streets or sidewalks of the city." Utah Code Annotated 10-8-76

The above picture "Kinderspeel" done in the 17th century depicts at least eleven violations according to the state statutes listed in this section.

The problem of specificity in determining who, in fact, has broken the law is exemplified by the disparity between the general statute of Hillsborough County, New Hampshire, and the detail of New Orleans City, Louisiana:

Hillsborough, N.H.:

The statute (RSA 644:2 II E) makes it a violation for a person who with a purpose of causing public inconvenience, annoyance or alarm or recklessly creating a risk thereof, obstructs vehicular or pedestrian traffic. Moreover, paragraph IV of TSA 644:2 makes disorderly conduct a misdemeanor if the offense continues after a request by any person to desist. Penalties for being convicted of a violation may be probation, conditional or unconditional discharge and a fine of up to $100.00. Penalties for a misdemeanor is a fine of up to $1,000, probation for two years, and incarceration for one year.

New Orleans, La.:

Section 38-127. Use of coasters, roller skates, and similar devices restricted.

No person upon roller skates or riding in or by means of any coaster, toy vehicle or similar device or hand-propelled vehicle shall go upon any roadway except while crossing a street on a crosswalk and when so crossing such person shall be granted all the rights and shall be subject to all of the duties applicable to pedestrians.

In either case, a roller skater can be thrown in jail, but the former leaves room for constitutional debate. Also an ordinance of New Orleans is:

Section 38-128. Clinging to moving vehicles.

No person riding upon any bicycle, coaster, sled, roller skates or vehicle shall attach it or himself to any streetcar or moving vehicle upon any roadway.

(This would greatly disappoint people like Paul Anka had he lived farther South:)

I was born and raised in Ottawa, Canada - July 30, 1941. As far back as I can remember, winter always made a large impression on me. It was always very cold and a lot of snow covered the ground for many months. One of our favorite "outings" was called "bunking." One's credentials had to be a pair of good leather gloves and heavy soled snow shoes -- and a pair of strong arms. You can well imagine, with all the snow, how slick the surface became on the streets. A bus would pass our local hangout, which was "George's Corner Store," every ten minutes making a stop at the bus hut on the corner. My friends and I would hide behind the hut, wait for the bus to make the stop and as it continued on it's way, we would run out from behind the hut, latch on to the back bumper (assuming a bending position) and hitch a free ride for about a mile. When we got to the other end, we would wait for the next bus coming back.

Sincerely,

Paul Anka

PAUL ANKA

Many district attorneys across the country expressed the opinion that street games are rarely a problem in themselves. In Wyoming, the City Attorney reported that Cheyenne "is located on the wide plains with plenty of game area, and street games like football have not been much of a problem." In fact, many cities, particularly those with dense population (including New York, Philadelphia, Albuquerque, Portland and Seattle), have written codes stressing the need for playing in the streets. In King County (Seattle, Washington), code 47.36.060-4 entitled "Play Streets" reads:

Whenever authorized signs are erected indicating any street or part thereof as a play street, no person shall drive a vehicle upon any such street or portion thereof except operators of vehicles having business or whose residences are within such closed area, and then any said operator shall exercise the greatest care in driving upon any such street or portion thereof.

Whatever the concerns, the laws, or the protection, the conclusion that seems most apparent is that there is no agreement among the fifty states as to what constitutes the precautionary exercise of these ends, though street games (and inconsistency) reign supreme throughout the country.

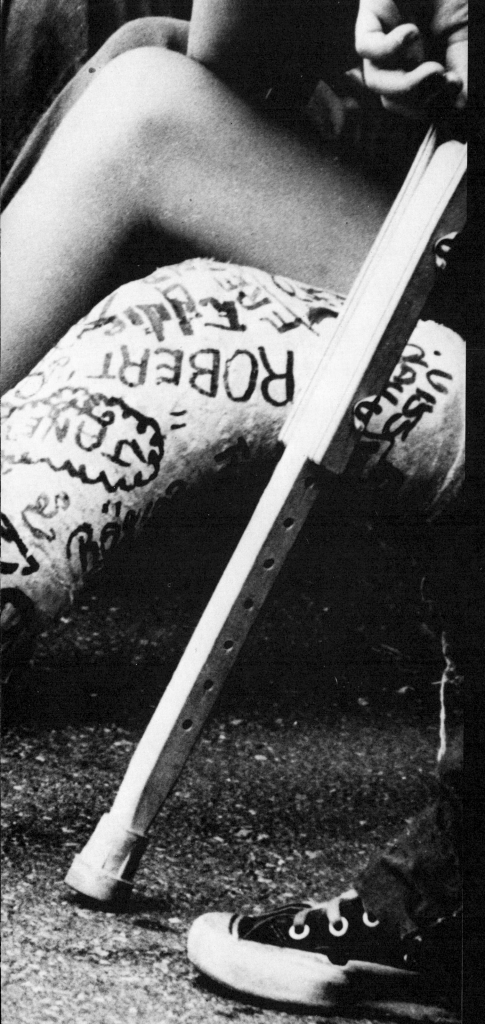

The 4th Quarter

DIVERSIONS

Flipping Cards
Chicken
Garbage Pail Basketball
Boxball, Four Square
Red Light–Green Light
Concentration, Thumper,
 Indian Chief
Spud
Patty Cake
Stoopball, Curb Ball,
 Night Ball, Roofing
Skelly
Territory, Land
Keep Away
Frisbee

THE GAME MAP

FADS, *Diversions,*

There are many amusements, some chaotic, others organized, that cannot be clearly classified as street games -- though they are games and ones that are very much a part of street life.

There are many goal-oriented games: School, House, Store -- and last but far from least, Doctor. Discovery, a major element in Doctor, also prevails in kissing games, word games, and puzzles. Discovering one's own ability to solve problems and conquer the odds is as important as discovering one's own body or that of the opposite sex. The other "pretending" games -- House, School, etc., find their truest place as one escape from the games of competition. They are often played on the sidewalk or, as in Doctor, a dark corner, alley, or quiet garage, where patient care and privacy can be maximized. All these games are limited only by the wildness of the imagination, while they relieve everyday anxieties and tensions.

Another type of less strenuous game is collecting match book covers, rocks, beer cans, tin foil and trash. These activities are bound by some dimension of reality, making them less palatable over a sustained period of time, but still others involve psycho-drama, as Carol Burnett suggested, adding zest to the more regular "institutional-pretending" games.

There are quiet games which encourage individual achievement -- for example, building chains out of gum wrappers or soda-pop snaps. Paper chains, yo-yo's, boomerangs, fli-back balls, kite-flying, tops, all emphasize individual skill and leave room in which an individual can achieve excellence. All these achievement games also are fads -- a fad being a game that has an enthusiastic, but temporary, following. Such games of the street come, go, and return, forming a complete cycle.

My favorite game when I was a kid was acting out
jungle movies. I went to the movies with my Grandmother
every Saturday, and when we got home I'd get all the
kids together on a vacant lot, and we'd do our version
of the movie. I'm sorry I don't have any pictures of
any of this. It was great fun. My pretty cousin would
always be the heroine. I always wound up being Tarzan,
or someone like that.

Sincerely,

Carol Burnett

M.M. (Mary Martin)

H.H. (Hubert Humphrey)

In quiet moments pets are a favorite diversion.

Norman Rockwell and his brother

..tell you the truth, I started illustrating
when I was 18 and I went to art school
before that. As a child I was drawing instead of playing games with the other
children.

Sincerely yours,

Norman
Rockwell

HAND GAMES

X marks the spot
With a dot dot dot
A squeeze here
A squeeze there
A bit of the air.

Here's the church,
Here's the steeple,
Open the doors
And see the people.

(religious handy work)

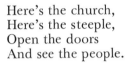

Helen Hayes playing house

I know nothing about your subject matter. At the age of four and five, due to family necessity, my beloved sister, Dorothy, and I were put to work in the theatre, consequently as children we never experienced "street games."

Most earnestly,

Lillian Gish
Lillian Gish

Unlike most children, I was writing a newspaper as a kid. I also produced and acted in a movie and was a cartoonist. I really didn't have the time to play the usual children's street games.

Hugh Hefner

It was taken at a track meet in back of my father's studio when I was 13 years old.

Yours sincerely,

Douglas Fairbanks

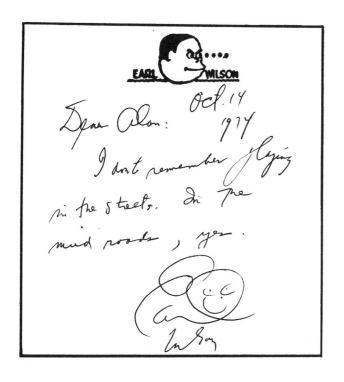

EARL WILSON

Dear Alan: Oct. 14
1974

I don't remember flying
in the streets. In the
mud roads, yes.

Hyperventilating (right).

Building pyramids (below).

I didn't play many games when I was a young girl. I wasn't good
at them or so I thought—BUT!—there was a pond across the road
from our summer house and ten or fifteen of us would gather after
swimming and look for sleeping water snakes that lived among the
rocks. We often would see them, small heads, beady eyes, slithering
through the black water as we swam . . .
When we found one coiled and quiet among the rocks, one of the
boys (it was always a boy) reached down, grabbed him by his tail,
whirled him round and round over his head and splat the snake's
head down on a boulder about five feet from the pond.
That was the most exciting game I can think of. Once a month
during the summer, the police patrol would pull up and with their
guns shoot maybe four or five that were swimming. Later on, one
of them told us they had shot water moccasins— now they are
dangerous . . . we didn't play that game anymore . . . and we only
swam when it was very hot.

Tammy Grimes 1975

> *When I was a child my favorite playmates were paper dolls and any other kind of dolls. With them I could have an imaginary world and play for hours by myself.*
>
> *Sincerely,*
>
> *Barbara Walters*

Louis Nizer

Unfortunately, I don't have any pictures and, in any case, wouldn't have any playing games - I spent all of my time at the movies.

Sincerely,

Walter Kerr
xx

Thumb Wrestling

Flipping Cards

ORIGIN:

Although baseball cards are the beloved "tickets" for trading, matching, or flipping—Elvis, Steve McQueen, the Osmonds, Davy Crockett, and the Beatles have all had a special place in the hearts of the "cardsharks" of yesteryear. One of the earliest picture fads was that of the movie stars on the underside of Dixie Cup covers. One simply licked off the cover to see what star he got.

Baseball cards, however, even preceded licking lids. The first baseball card was produced in 1886 and sold as an insert in a pack of cigarettes. After Old Judge Cigarettes issued the cards, other tobacco companies soon followed suit. Around 1910, companies such as Tip Top Bread and Cracker Jack hopped on the bandwagon of companies already printing cards.

After a temporary recession in card enthusiasm from 1916-1932, the bubble gum card burst forth with a new era of hope. Several gum companies bubbled with sales until the outbreak of World War II. In 1948, the gum companies gave it another chew and the card rose to prominence once again. Companies such as Hunter's Weiners, Red Heart Dog Food, and Johnston Cookies have all issued cards, but the undeniable leader of the pack is Topps Chewing Gum. Since 1951, they have been issuing cards with statistics, autographs, and emblems. Though there are football cards, basketball cards, and hockey cards, baseball outsells any other by twice -- somewhere in the vicinity of 250 million a year.

Each player is photographed during the spring with and without his hat -- in case he is traded before the cards are finally issued. (This explains why some players are posed uncapped. For example, suppose Tom Seaver were wearing a NY cap and had become part of the Los Angeles Dodgers.) The company prints an equal number of cards of each player, regardless of popularity. Each player makes about $400.00 a year from his card, and each year there are 700 different cards offered.

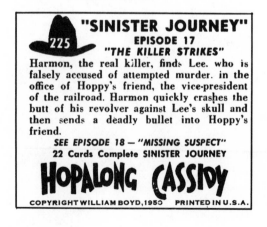

"Let's go, we got fighting to do!", Russel shouted. It wasn't easy for Davy to ride off and leave his wife and youngsters. But the Creek Indians had massacred every man, woman and child at Fort Mimms and the blood-thirsty warriors were getting too close for comfort. When Gen. Jackson asked for volunteers, Davy joined up—he knew this was his fight!

SEE CARD 3 – *"OFF TO BATTLE"*

10A *Beatles Diary*

Dear Diary,
John and I wrote SHE LOVES YOU in our hotel room last night. I don't think we won a popularity contest with the other guests, though. No matter how low we tried to sing, we kept disturbing someone. An elderly man pounded on the ceiling for about an hour to keep us quiet. Then someone next door yelled, "Shut Up."

Paul

©T.C.G.   PRINTED IN U.S.A.

CONGRESSMAN CROCKETT

MACK
DIESEL TRACTOR

HEAVY-DUTY TRUCK

America's Top Singer

Cards Courtesy of Topps Chewing Gum Co. Inc.

"TREASURE ... A Metro-Goldwyn-Mayer Picture
Playing in
JACKIE COOPER

"RIPTI... Metro-Goldwyn-Mayer Picture
Playing in
NORMA SHEARER

"GABRIEL OVER TH... A Metro-Goldwyn-Mayer Picture
Playing in
DICKIE MOORE

"A WOMAN IN HER THIRTIES" ... A Warner Bros. Picture
Playing in
ANN DVORAK

Playing in Columbia Pictures
EDMUND LOWE

"CLEOPATRA" ... A Paramount Picture
Playing in
CLAUDETTE COLBERT

"YOU'RE TELLING ME" ... A Paramount Picture
Playing in
LARRY (BUSTER) CRABBE

"DINNER AT EIGHT" ... A Metro-Goldwyn-Mayer Picture
Playing in
JEAN HARLOW

"HE WAS HER MAN" ... A Warner Bros. Picture
Playing in
JAMES CAGNEY

"SADIE McKEE" ... A Metro-Goldwyn-Mayer Picture
Playing in

"WE'RE NOT DRESSING" ... A Paramount Picture
Playing in

"THE FIREBRAND" ... A Twentieth Century Production
Playing in

O'DAY, P. Washington

CARL HUBBELL

BALL

DOMINICK DiMAGGIO

Standing only 5'9", the Boston Red Sox center-fielder smacked American League pitching in 1950 for a .328 average

No. 20 IN A SERIES OF 52

1 SINGLE

ED LOPAT

Pitching his way to 18 wins the N.Y. Yanker southpaw curve baller was 6th in the AL with a 3.47 ERA last year

No. 39 IN 8 SERIES OF 52

SINGLE 1

DONALD LOUIS MOSSI

TOPPS 85

Height: 6'1"
Weight: 195
Throws: Left
Bats: Left
Home: Redwood City, Cal.
Born: Jan. 11, 1930

© T.C.G. printed in U.S.A.

A starting pitcher since he entered baseball in '49, Don switched to the bullpen last year with spectacular results. He led the League with the lowest Earned Run Average and posted the highest Won-Lost percentage! Always a Major League prospect Don had to overcome his wildness before making the grade. Ask any player if he succeeded—the answer's yes!

You're the UMP!

WHEN A BATTED BALL HITS THE PITCHER'S RUBBER AND BOUNCES FOUL, IS IT FAIR OR FOUL?

ANS. It is a foul ball.

MAJOR & MINOR LEAGUE PITCHING RECORDS

	Games	Innings	Won	Lost	Pct.	Hits	Runs	E.R.	S.O.	Walks	E.R.Avg.
Year	40	93	6	1	.857	56	22	20	55	39	1.94
*Life	170	916	54	46	.540	824	444	360	678	476	3.54

GIANTS

John McGraw

OF THE NEW YORK NATIONALS

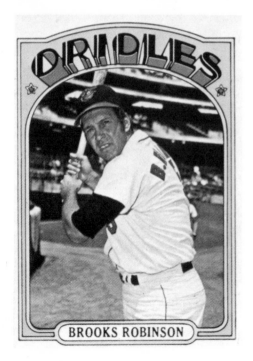

ORIOLES

BROOKS ROBINSON

MATHEWSON, N.Y. NAT'L

AARON

1962   1963
1964   HANK AARON SPECIAL   1965

BRAVES

HANK AARON

EQUIPMENT:

Today one can easily obtain a starter set of cards by buying a packet of bubble gum at the local candy store. Inside the waxed paper wrapper will be eight cards of living baseball players. Also enclosed, for the nostalgia buffs, is one stick of compressed gum (which can easily be shattered with a hard, sharp object). The cards smell like the gum (and the gum tastes like the cardboard). One is better off chewing the cards, but most collectors, who are usually in the range of seven to fourteen years old, care very little about the gum. It's the cards they're after.

OBJECTIVE:

To win and hoard as many cards as there are in the neighborhood.

RULES:

Game I--Flipping

Every card, like every coin, has two sides, and this game closely patterns flipping coins (as in Heads or Tails). The front, or "head," of the card has a photograph of a player printed in early color-TV hues, and the back, or "tail," has a series of invaluable statistics.

Two players or flippers mutually agree on how many cards should be flipped before the game gets under way. Once the agreement is reached, one player flips the designated number of cards. The next player in line tries to match the pattern, be it two heads and a tail, or three heads, etc. If he matches the pattern exactly, he wins all the cards, and if not, he forfeits them all to his opponent's growing collection (assuming his opponent is a proficient card-flipper).

Pointers on Flipping: A good player should hold the edges of the card between the forefinger on one side of the card and the thumb on the other. He then gently brings back his forearm, past his side, and with an equally gentle movement, brings the card forward, snapping his wrist at the moment of release. The action is similar to throwing a bowling ball, but in this case weighing only half an ounce. There is occasionally a scientist among flippers who claims that a gentle thrust of a card, picture side up, will always land as a tail. It has been tried but never proven.

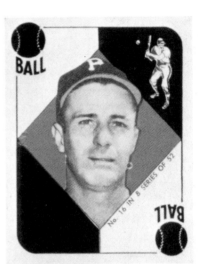

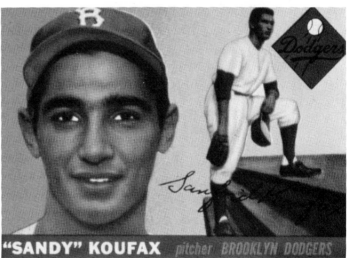

Most valuable card in the world Honus Wagner. This is one of six or seven cards left, each valued at $1,500.

Game II--Pitching

This is the gambler's dream -- or nightmare -- win or lose all. The idea of the game is to throw the card as close to a specified line or wall as possible. One player draws a line six-to-ten feet from, and parallel to, the target line or wall. Each player then shoots four or five cards from the drawn line, alternating turns between each shot. Whoever gets his card closest wins the whole pile. Any card that touches the line or wall is a "killer" or a "spiker" -- unbeatable unless another card is pitched on top of it. The sure win is to shoot a card so that it leans at an angle against a wall. No fast talk can change the fact that a leaner is a sure thing!

Pitching Pointers: A perfect pitcher squats down low, card between thumb and forefinger, and sends it forward with a snap of the wrist. Here the action is like throwing a low-level Frisbee. It is important to stay low in order to

avoid unwanted wafts of wind. Finally, the prudent player keeps his eye on the shooting, or starting, line -- any observant opponent will surely notice if his foot should go over. In case of a foot fault, any opponent will notify the pitcher of his mistake in an atonal shriek.

Game III--Off the Wall

Unlike the other two games, this variation was rarely played with Dixie Cup covers, since they are unevenly weighted. Any number can play this version of the game, which simply involves each player in trying to drop his card on another player's card from a certain height. One player holds his cards against the wall at a specific height and lets go. Then it is in the hands of the gods. If it lands on top of any card, the player takes all at the end of the match -- unless topped by one of the players following him.

Game IV--Trading

In actuality, this is anything but a game. Early childhood greed is expressed in the piles of baseball cards stuffed in the drawers of a collector's room. One carefully weighs, in the process of trading, every deal, even if it's six players who stink for one Willie Mays. Not until the early collector reaches adult life does he get into the trading of past cards. As far as the young trader is concerned, last year's player is as good as dead (though there is some recent evidence that this trend is changing).

WORLD FACTS AND RECORDS

Largest Collection -- The late Jefferson Burdick of Syracuse, New York, had over 200,000 cards covering the 1880's up through the 1950's, when he donated his collection to the Museum of Modern Art.

Most Valuable Card -- Honus Wagner (six in existence).

Chicken

ORIGIN:

Chicken is an old game called by many different names. However, anyone who ends up being marked "chicken" knows exactly what that means -- whatever the name of the game.

The game thrives on an underlying sentiment, appealing more to the rule: "It's more fun to do what you're not supposed to do" than the reverse. Running around a pool instead of walking, jumping down the stairs, using a roof as a boardwalk instead of an overhead shelter, filling balloons with water rather than air, and running up the down escalator -- all fall within this realm. The environment and local customs are often reflected in such risk-taking ventures.

By any standard, they are a test of nerve and peer-pressure where "babies" who back down are cowards and "grown-ups" who go through with it are courageous. Even without close observation, the unquenchable thirst for doing "no-no's" is far removed from mature behavior. In fact, any adult aware that his kid is doing the things he did in childhood is aghast -- "I'd kill him if he did the things I did!" is the usual comment.

> One of my favorite pastimes was playing jokes on cars. My friends and I would dress up dummies—that is one slip cover from a piece of furniture—and stuff a pillow or two into them. Then a paper bag filled with rags was used for a head and on rainy days we put a raincoat on the dummy. They were all pretty close to life size. The fun of the game was to throw out the human look-alike in front of a passing car. Great fun!
>
> *Anthony Perkins*

OBJECTIVE:

To live as long as possible and still be accepted by friends.

RULES (so to speak):

The first game to be played is Truth or Dare, which is a mild form of Chicken. A group of boys or girls gathers in an enclosed area discussing different possibilities for consequences. The only safeguard against total cruelty is the fact that any player is vulnerable before the game actually begins. Therefore, he is careful not to make the consequences too severe, knowing he may end up the final victim.

Once a consequence, such as a player having to run around the block backwards, make a phony phone call to a teacher, or tell a girl he likes her (or vice versa), is worked out by unanimous consent, the game is on its way. The format is much like group "I've Got a Secret," where one person is asked to tell a secret. Failure to tell the truth results in a dare (the consequence).

It is a popular game until a dangerous version of Follow the Leader emerges as the next step to excitement and challenge. Here, the leader selects certain feats or dares without necessarily having to perform them first himself, unless he is a fool. The less hazardous favorites first:

The player hails a cab, opens the door, walks through, and out the other side. If the cab driver catches him, he's in bad shape.   Along the same lines, there is the congenial, "What does your father do?" dare. In this verbal hit-and-run, two players stand by a uniformed worker, i.e., a policeman. One asks the other, "What does your father do?" loudly enough to catch the policeman's attention. The other replies, "He doesn't work; he's a cop," and they both run.

The yen for excitement, humiliation, torture, and danger provides the stimulus for new and formal games requiring strong skulls and nerve fibre.

SCORING:

Though no player knows exactly why, there seems to be nothing worse than being called a chicken or sissy. The marked individual tries to escape the trauma and the street on which he lives. He yearns to grow up quickly, break the stigma of his reputation, and rush away good years, unaware that there is another street just around the corner.

VARIATIONS:

Chinese Fire Drill

A vehicle stops at a traffic light and the challenged player runs around the car hollering, kicking the tires, and banging on the windows as many times as he can until the light changes. The player who runs around the car the most times before the driver gets out of his car, wins.

Bikes

This is a take-off on Ivanhoe and the jousting of the Middle Ages. Two bike riders station themselves at opposite ends of the block and proceed to head into each other. The one who steers away first from the collision course is proclaimed "chicken." In some cases, pride prevails until the moment of impact, by Gulliver! It is unlikely that this game will ever be endorsed by the President's Council on Physical Fitness.

Joe Namath, tricycling at a very early age, 3 to be exact.

Garbage Pail Basketball

ORIGIN:

The Mayan played with a rubber ball and stone hoops somewhat along the lines of basketball. Courts have been found throughout Central America. The stakes of the game were rather different from those today -- a bit of strip poker and decapitation, depending on who won, were all part of the Mayan sport.

Several hundred years later, James Naismith, a professor at the YMCA Training College in Springfield, Massachusetts, set out to devise a game similar in principle. In 1891, he formalized a game of passing a ball, utilizing speed and agility, without physical contact or decapitation between opponents, and called it Basketball.

The garbage pail, the other ingredient in the game, was invented* and manufactured in this country around 1907, in West Virginia, for the sole purpose of collecting trash.

Little did anyone know that the game of the Mayan and Dr. Naismith would be adapted to the streets, or that the garbage pail would become a collector of balls. There are over 80 countries playing basketball under the official rules. In the unofficial arena, where there are basketballs and trash (which includes most countries), there's a good chance this hybrid will be in the forefront of community play. The game thrives in cities where hoops cannot be built or afforded and where a spontaneous game is desired. In the United States alone, over 25,000 tons of steel were used to make 5,000,000 garbage pails last year. The cities having the greatest density in population and thus garbage, such as New York, Chicago, and Los Angeles, have the best Garbage Pail Basketball teams.

* inventor wished to remain anonymous

Holyoke Basketball Team

EQUIPMENT:
    1 basketball
    1 garbage pail (preferably empty) or
    1 fire escape ladder (see photo - step of ladder as hoop)

OBJECTIVE:
    To put the ball in the garbage pail which is guarded by the opposing team. (Years back, a fruit basket was used, but wooden baskets and crates become scarcer each year.)

RULES:
Two or more players can play the game, which has only one pail sitting on the curb, a shrine in city life. Most often, the garbage pail is placed near a hydrant, an area supposedly free of cars. The fifteen feet of open space on both sides of the hydrant define the sidelines of the court. When cars are illegally parked, they define the sidelines. The center, or starting, line is in the middle of the street, and the end line is delineated by the cars parked across the street. The major changes from the official rules are the elimination of: a second basket on the opposite side of the court, a flat court surface, a suspended hoop, and physical contact.

Once the teams are chosen and who gets the ball first is decided, the game begins. The team carrying the ball must always pass or dribble the ball once they have taken it past the middle of the road (center line). The opposing team can block any player from shooting the ball, as long as there is no physical contact. However, this never occurs, and a foul is called--usually a reference to the court language. Any player hit, who can get off the ground, can take a foul shot from the center line or sewer, if he's lucky enough to be in front of the pail.

If the ball is intercepted during a pass, or is retrieved by the defending team after the shot misses the pail, the ball is theirs.

However, they must bring the ball back past the middle of the road before they can shoot a pail. If someone makes a pail, then the ball goes to the defending team. This alternates each time one team makes a garbage pail.

Should the ball be hit out of bounds by a defending player, the ball is played from wherever it left the street while in the hands of the offense. When a passer or dribbler lets the ball out of bounds himself, he forfeits the ball to the other team.

SCORING:

Every pail made scores two points, and every successful foul shot is worth one point. Very often referees aren't available and everyone depends on the word of the person who was fouled, slugged, tripped, or punched. If someone calls a foul and is not visibly wounded, debate is sure to arise. Therefore, minor technicalities, such as holding, touching, goosing, or psyching-out an opponent are overlooked for more serious foul play. There is no time limit, and most players sweat and pant into the wee hours of the night. Once everyone reaches a reasonable level of exhaustion, the team with the highest number of points wins.

Left: Mayan stone-carving

DIAGRAM

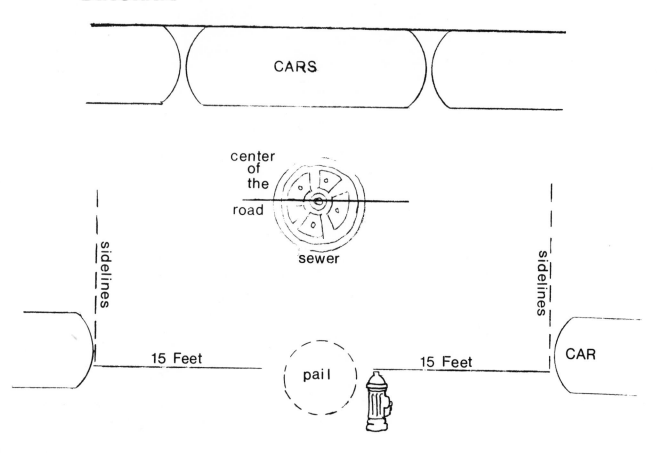

VARIATIONS:

Twenty-one

A game of shooting pails from the middle of the road. Each person shoots until he misses. When someone misses, the ball goes to the next person. All points, or pails, are cumulative, with the first person to reach twenty-one pails the winner.

Horse

This is for the shooting connoisseur. One player displays a skillful left- or right-hook, running lay-down (remember, the pail is below the player), foul or long shot. If he misses the pail, the next player can choose his favorite strategy, and so it goes with each succeeding turn. But, if the shot goes in, every player must follow, perfectly matching the shot, from the exact same place. Whoever fails, gets the letter "H," until one player has at least five such failures, spelling H-O-R-S-E and "loser," at the same time.

Boxball and 4-Square

ORIGIN:

    The street version of Boxball, or Slug, has a heritage of Handball and Sloth. These two gave rise to the game in the beginning of the 20th century.

EQUIPMENT:

    chalk or white adhesive tape or paint
    1 handball or spaldeen
    2 human beings

OBJECTIVE:

    To hit the ball into an opponent's box in the hope that he won't return it. Without rackets, it's handy work all the way.

RULES:

Street—The court should be twenty- by thirty-feet, with a center line giving each man a box twenty- by fifteen-feet. Tape, chalk, or paint are good ways to lay out the court.

    The server, standing behind the serving line, smacks the ball over the center line into his opponent's box. The player receiving the ball runs into his court and hits the ball back after one bounce or on the fly. The ball must be returned the same way each time. The play continues until one player fails to return the ball properly or hits it out of bounds.

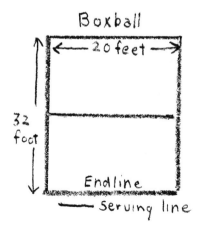

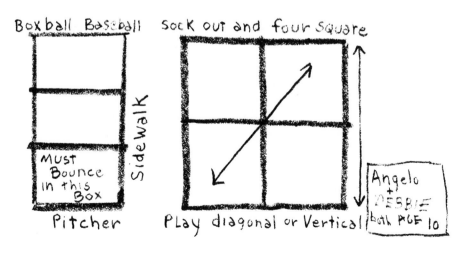

Sidewalk—Close observation reveals that a cement sidewalk with carefully masoned lines, is divided into boxes. One person stands behind the line of the box or sidewalk square--rectangle, to be exact--while the other challenger stands behind the same line, one box away and opposite his opponent. The game is very much like table tennis without the net, table, paddle, or ping-pong ball. All the rules of the street version apply here, except that a ball hitting the cement center line is considered fair play.

SCORING:

Only the serving side or server scores. One point is made each time his opponent fails to return the ball properly or just fails to return the ball at all. If the server improperly returns the ball, or errs in any way, the ball is lost to his opponent, who then becomes the server. Eleven points wins the game.

Boxball Baseball

An additional sidewalk square separates the players in this version. One player is the batter and the other, pitcher, outfielder, first, second, and third baseman, as well as shortstop. This makes team effort an essential path to victory. Commonly, players take the identity of a professional team to give the game panache. It was the Yankees versus the Brooklyn Dodgers, if you were from New York and over 30, and the Mets versus the Los Angeles Dodgers, if you're under 20 and from California.

Every pitcher, regardless of his team, must throw the ball so that it bounces in the box farthest from him. There are no balls and no strikes. When the batter hits a good pitch into the third box (from where he's standing), and the pitcher catches the ball on one bounce, it's a single. It's a double on the second bounce and a triple on the third. If the ball is caught without a bounce, the batter flies out. Any ball hit outside the third box is also an out. Three outs, and the side retires; the batter and pitcher switch places. The game is over after nine innings as in standard baseball.

Four-Square or Sock-Out

In the absence of sidewalks, a two- or four-box square is chalked out on the street. The game is similar to boxball, except for a unique language which dictates the type of ball hitting permitted in the game. Here are some examples:

Tea-party--light bouncing of the ball between the boxes.
War -- hitting the ball as hard as possible.
Block--stopping the ball with one's palm, letting it drop and bounce, then returning it.
Skimmer--rubbing one's knuckles on the ground before returning the ball. This type of ball travels close to the ground.
Skyiers Ba-Boing -- Smashing the ball straight down in one's own box with the shameful risk of its bouncing back into your own box.

Once the language is learned, the leader, or winner from a previous game, states the rules before any playing begins. "No teaparties, wars, or blocks," is stated strictly at the discretion of the leader, while doing a jig in the four squares.

The final part of the ritual is called "cementing in the rules." Once the leader specifies what should or should not be included in the game, he sings, "Crisscross applesauce," doing another jig, cementing in the rules. Then the game proceeds as Boxball. In Four-Square, the ball can be hit to the opponent directly opposite or diagonally opposite.

Any special hitting method can be used to give the game variation, with the general purpose of just trying to get the ball past an opponent. If the ball is caught, the game is lost. In *Curves,* the ball is given a back-spin with the slice of the palm by the pitcher (see Flukes). In *Up and Over,* the ball must be stopped with the palm, hit up in the air, letting it fall to the ground and take one bounce before it is hit back into the other box. It must be returned in exactly the same way. The method of scoring is left to the whim of the players.

Flukes

Fluking is a method of throwing and curving a spaldeen. Releasing the ball from the hand, palms facing upward, gives it a top-spin which upon bouncing, speeds quickly forward. Releasing the ball, knuckles out, renders an under-spin, sending the ball backward once it hits the ground. When possible, a right- or left-spin can be put on the ball by crushing the pinky between one finger and throwing the ball to the left or right, respectively. The basic thrust of fluking is to confuse an opponent after the ball bounces in front of him.

Red Light

OBJECTIVE:

A group of players (cars) try to overcome a human street light.

My favorite yard game is "Redlight". Alot of childen can play it. One person is that Redlight. The Redlight turns his back to rereyone way on the other side of the yard. He says one-two-three redlight and turns around fast. But when he was turned everyone moved closer and froze in thier footsteps. If the Redlight sees you moving he makes you go all the way back to the beginning. The first one to touch him when his back is turned wins the game and gets to be the Redlight.
It's fun to be the Redlight. It makes me giggle to see All the funny faces and positions. Play it sometime! Denette

Cowen
Age 8

Green Light

ORIGIN:

Red Light-Green Light was surely a European import, played as it is in its present form as early as 1890. In Europe, it is commonly called, "Peep Behind the Curtain" and in "you know where" -- Peep Behind the Iron Curtain.

The first electric street lights blinked red and green in 1919 on the sidewalks of New York. This, in addition to the fact that the game is played in the street, struck a logical chord in American Youth who named the game Red Light-Green Light. (In addition to which, one would be more apt to find a red light on the street than a curtain.) In Hungary, the game is called "Cat and Mice," and in Germany, "Oxen."

RULES:

Two or more people can play, though less than four people makes for a draggy game. One member volunteers to be the light. This seems to be the more honored role in the game, so there is little hesitation on the part of the participants to offer their services.

"1-2-3 Red Light"

Once that's out of the way, the rest of the group gives a gentle grunt of dissatisfaction that each of them was not chosen as the light, as they mope over to one side of the street. When the game is played in a schoolyard, the group is about twenty feet from the light.

When everyone is in position, the light turns his face to the wall of a building and starts the action with the words, "Green Light." The runners, or cars, speedily move toward the light, never knowing when the light will turn around, yelling, "Red Light," at which time all cars must brake to a full stop. If one solitary part of their anatomy is moving, be it fender, tail pipe, or blinker, they must shift gears and go back to the starting line. In some areas, it is a pre-determined number of steps backward (mileage).

A runner must be sly and a bit lucky if he wants to avoid turning back his odometer each turn by outfoxing the light. Some runners move gently forward at each turn with a secure sense of their braking power. Yet others, whether or not they are equipped with power brakes (sneakers), run forward full blast and couldn't possibly stop, even with a five-minute warning. Since the object is to reach and tag the changing light, a happy medium between both speeds is necessary.

Each time the light turns back to the wall, or changes to green, the advance continues. Whoever reaches the light first becomes the next light. In theory, the light is supposed to count to ten before saying red light while turning around to face the oncoming traffic. In practice, the numbers are counted off with computer-like speed, inaudible even to a dog's ears. The light often yells "Red Light," before he's even begun to turn around.

Generally, it is easy to hear the first and the last part of the count, "1-2-#&&#%%&-RED LIGHT." Some neighborhoods, aware of this syndrome, have simply shortened it to "1-2-3 Red Light." Even then, as the cars approach the light, the words accelerate until only "1" and "light" are audible. Everyone cheated!

Concentration, Thumper and Indian Chief

OBJECT:

To perform a series of feats in rapid succession with each player in a circle trying to eliminate the other until only one remains.

RULES:

Concentration

The group sits in a circle and counts off consecutive numbers. Then the circle is set in motion. Everyone slaps thighs, claps hands, snaps the fingers on the left hand and then the right -- each motion follows the next in a rhythmic pattern. The overall pattern is done in unison.

On the snap of the left finger, one player calls off his own number and on the snap of the right, the number of another player, something like: slap, clap, three (snap), one (snap), in time to the pace set by the entire circle. Slap, clap, snap, snap continues (with the roll call) until one player misses his beat, call, or calls a number of someone previously eliminated. The person who erred steps out of the circle, and the beat goes on.

An increased tempo forces faster thinking and consequently more mistakes.

For variety, different categories, such as movie stars, colors, hygienic terminology, can be substituted for numbers. Each person on the circle must render, in turn, a response in the category being played. The name must come on the two snap beats. If a player can't think fast enough or has run out of names or fouls up the beat on his turn, he's out. The person to the right of the one who blundered sets the next category and the beat. The winner is the last person left reciting names in a specific category.

INDIAN CHIEF
By Susan
(Age 11)

Thumper

This quasi-adult version of Concentration eliminates the rhythm method in favor of fast brain action. If there is any relationship between maturity and brightness, there is no evidence of that in this game. Counting numbers has been dropped and, instead all the players are assigned specific gestures--a slap in the face, hitting the forehead, a wink, sticking out the tongue, a clap, crossing the eyes, touching the nose--the possibilities are only limited by inhibition.

Each player's gesture remains his stigma for the whole of the game. The difficulty lies in remembering everyone's idiosyncracy while playing the game. Once joined in a circle, one member asks the traditional opening question, "What's the name of the game?" The group responds, "Thumper," pounding their fists rapidly against the floor or ground. (God knows why.) One player does his symbol, followed by symbol or gesture of another player, i.e., a hit in the head and a finger in the nose. Then whoever is finger-in-the-nose, puts his finger in his nose and follows with a new gesture. All the players carefully watch the person performing, anticipating their own turns. The gestures fly randomly around the circle until someone fouls up.

Teenagers and college students play Thumper with a keg of beer nearby. Everytime a player is eliminated, everyone takes a swig of beer. Ultimately, each player gets more and more woozy, until he can't remember who's out, can't even recognize the person next to him, never mind the symbol. No one is sober enough to find out who the winner is until the next morning -- and by that time, no one cares.

Indian Chief

This is a pre-schooler novelty. One member of the circle leaves, while another member is chosen chief. The excluded youngster returns to the room, unaware of who is leading the group in a series of motions -- clapping hands, rubbing tummies, pounding feet, etc. The chief decides what activity the circle should pursue, and when he changes the action,everyone follows the change. Through keen observation, it is the task of the banished individual to determine which member of the circle is chief. If he guesses correctly, the chief is the next one sent from the room. Indian Chief is a game that can be highly recommended without reservation.

Spud

ORIGIN:

Though the exact origin is unclear, this cross between Ball Tag and Catch Ball seems to be uniquely American. The word "spud" means a spade-shaped knife, and if this is what early man played with, we've come a long way since them.

EQUIPMENT:

1 large ball (with good bounce) or a tennis ball for variation
5 or more human beings

OBJECTIVE:

To run toward or away from the spud throwing center, depending on which side of the ball you're on. Ultimately, the idea is not to get hit by the ball.

RULES:

Everyone gathers around the ball, or spud, throwing center. One person throws the ball high into the air, calling out the name of one of his fellow spudnicks. Whoever is named runs in to catch the descending ball while everyone else runs for his spudnick life.

Once the ball is caught, the catcher yells out SPUD!!! and all fleeing spudsters must freeze in their tracks. Then the caller is allowed to take four steps toward his chosen frozen victim (or spudcicle) before throwing the ball at him. If the victim is hit, he gets the letter "S." On the other hand, if the ball misses or is caught by the victim, the thrower gets the "S" instead. This continues until each member gets S-P-U-D and is out.

The group regathers after each shot. Whoever gets the letter is the new caller and can call anyone he wishes, including himself, if he wants to be a tricky spudster.

SCORING:

Each fault costs the player a letter. Four faults or letters spell S-P-U-D--and "you're out." The final player is the winner. One variation in scoring is: one fault equals one spud, three spuds and "you're out."

VARIATIONS:

Days of the Week

This is played with seven people, each taking on the name of a day of the week. One day of the week is shouted out instead of calling a friend's name.

I Declare War

Played exactly like Spud, except that each player is a country which has a piece of land chalked on the street around a sewer (see diagram). This mapping out of territory is strictly for positioning players, with no imperialistic motive intended. (No one *really* wants a piece of his friend's sewer.) The caller stands in the center, while all the others are around him in their geographic slices of the pie. The caller, or aggressor in this case, smashes his spalding against the sewer screaming, "I declare war on ..." naming the country of his choice. Then the game proceeds as in Spud.

DIAGRAM:

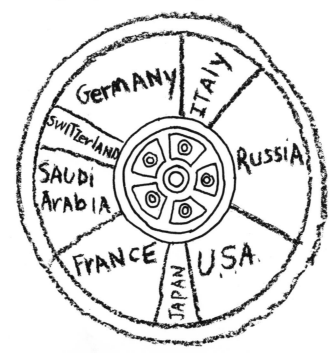

Patty Cake and Hand Clapping

ORIGIN:

Clapping chants appear in folklore of every continent around the globe. Europe (particularly Germany) and Asia have the greatest wealth of chants and have been the mainstream of clapping games. Almost all clapping chants have three beats in a two-pulse song and are frequently in 2/4 or 4/4 time.

EQUIPMENT:

Hands

OBJECTIVES:

To say or sing chants combined with different clapping patterns, at an increasing tempo, until the clapper falters, misses a beat, clap, or word.

Basic Clapping Pattern

1. *Each partner claps his own hands.*
2. *Partners clap hands together, palm-to-palm.*
3. *One person's hand claps the left hand of another person, then right.*
4. *One palm faces up, the other palm faces down. The partner's hands are in a reversed position.*

Patty Cake

Adults impress upon their babies or very young children the satisfaction they get from watching their offspring perform. Parents, uncles, aunts, grandmothers, grandfathers, etc., teach the wonder Patty Cake by singing the chant while forcing the child's hands together. (Baby seems to enjoy the struggles of his "teachers" as much as he does having his hands banged together.) In fact, one rarely hears anyone but an adult chant:

Patty cake, patty cake (force hands together)
Baker's man.
Make a cake
Just as fast as you can.
Roll it and pat it,
And mark it with "B". ("B" stands for baby)
And put it in the oven
For baby and me.

The child grows older and, hopefully, the adult outgrows the game. Young kids, however, retain some of the chant. The phrase, "patty cake, patty cake," is chanted to a variation on the Basic Clapping Pattern:

1,2,1 ... repeated infinitely with the words "patty cake." Repetition is the key to making any childhood song a "hit." Most adults later regret having taught the song, but by then it's too late. Eventually, even the chant is dropped, which is often a blessing, and a new pattern evolves:

1, 1, 2, 1, 3, 1, 2, 1, 3, etc.

Each round picks up speed until someone misses a clap or fouls up.

VARIATIONS:

Miss Mary Mack is the clap chant for the advanced clap-
per-slapper.

1—Cross hands over shoulders.
2—Slap knee.
3—Clap own hands together.
4—Clap partner's left hand first and then the right.

The rhythm and claps together:

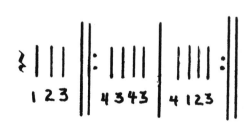

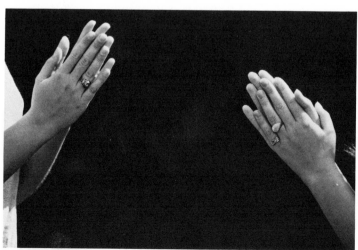

Miss Mary Mack, Mack, Mack,
Dressed in Black, Black, Black,
With silver buckles, buckles, buckles,
All down her back ,back, back.
She asked her mother for fifty cents
To see the elephants
Jump over the fence.
They jumped so high,
They reached the sky,
And never came down,
Till the Fourth of July.
(repeat chorus)
She went upstairs,
To say her prayers,
She bumped her head,
And now she's dead.

To add frivolity to this musical pastime, melody is added to some chants. This not only picks up the mood of the chant but also disguises the banality of the story line. The simplest song is:

Alabama, Mississippi, Alabama, New Orleans,
Alabama number one, you're gonna make it,
Make it, make it, make it baby.

The clapping pattern: 4, 2, 1, 4, 2, 1, etc.

Here's an example of what the media can do:

Winston tastes good like a cigarette should
Winston tastes good like a oo-ah...
I wanna piece of pie ,pie too sweet.
I wanna piece of meat, meat too tough.
I wanna ride a bus, bus too full.
I wanna ride a bull ,bull too black.
I wanna go back.

Then there are some standard tunes from the clapping hit parade.

Down, Down Baby (four beats and a snap of the finger to each measure)

Down, down, baby.
Down by the roller coaster.
Sweet, sweet baby.
I don't want to let you go.
Shimmy, Shimmy cocoa pop.
Shimmy, shimmy, pop.
Please mister postman,
Don't let me do the
Shimmy, shimmy cocoa pop.
Shimmy, shimmy pop. (hit your partner on pop)

Two Lips

Just face two lips together,
Tie them together.
Bring back my love to me.
What is the meaning,
Of all these daisies?
This is my story, the story of love,
From me to you.
My heart goes bumpity-ya-ta,
Bumpity ya ta over the deep blue sea.
What is the meaning of all these daisies?
This is the story, the story of love ,
From me to you.
Cha cha cha.

Johnny Over the Ocean

Johnny over the ocean,
Johnny over the sea,
Johnny broke a saucer,
Blamed it on me.
I told Ma, Ma told Pa,
And Johnny got a lickin ,ha, ha, ha.
(repeat with Johnny broke a bottle, pitcher, lightbulb, etc.)
Poor clutzy Johnny.

And perhaps the classic clap of all times, *Miss Lucy:*

Lucy had a steamboat, steamboat had a bell,
Steamboat went to heaven and Lucy went to ...
Hell-o operator, give me number nine,
If you disconnect me, I'll chop off your ...

Behind the refrigerator, there was a piece of glass,
And if you don't like it, you can just ...
Ask me no more questions, tell me no more lies,
The boys are in the bathroom pulling down their ...
Flies are in the garbage, bees are in the park,
Boys and girls are kissing in the dark dark, dark
Ask me no more questions, tell me no more lies (refrain)
A man got hit with a bottle of pop, right between the eyes.

For an encore this verse is added:

Lucy had a baby, she named him tiny Tim.
She put him in the bathtub to see if he could swim.
He drank up all the water, he ate up all the soap,
He tried to eat the bathtub, but it wouldn't go down his throat.
Miss Lucy called a doctor, etc. etc. etc.

until the imagination runs out of ideas.

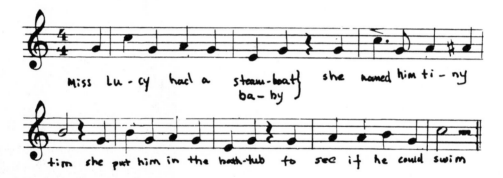

There are also clapping chants that abruptly end in some form of physical torture. In the song "Spads," one of three verdicts; Chocolate—a slap, Vanilla—a fist, or Strawberry—a tickle, is delivered on the last line of the song.

The spads go Anna banana
Plays the piana.
All she can play is
The Star Spangled Banna.
Anna Banana split (then the verdict).

The final illustration accents the vast differences between a song sung in both urban and rural America. Black and white, North and South are also important factors that contribute to the rhythm, accent, tempo, and content of the songs.

Ol' Little Playmate

Rural

Question:
Ol' little playmate
Come out and play with me,
And bring your dollies three.
Climb up my apple tree.   *(rural reply)*
Slide down my rainbow,
Onto my cellar door.   *Ol' little playmate,*
And we'll be jolly friends,   *I cannot play with you*
Forever, more more ,more.   *My dolly has the flu,*
     Boo hoo ,hoo, hoo.

Urban

Question:
Ol' little devil
Come out an fight with me
I'll scratch your eyeballs out.
I'll push you out the window,   *(urban reply)*
Onto my cellar floor.
I'll push you in the mud.   *I cannot come out and fight with you*
And we'll be jolly enemies,   *My enemy's got the flu,*
Forever more ,more more.   *Yeah, yeah, yeah, yeah.*

Stoopball, Curbball, Nightball, and Roofing

ORIGIN:

All four games take their ancestry from Townball, an early attempt at Baseball. But Stoopball owes its uniqueness to the emergence of the Brownstone. The Dutch *stoep* was brought into New Amsterdam by Dutch settlers in New York City in 1783. Though the stoop was originally of Greek design, the traditional flooding of the Netherlands explains their adoption there. At the time of their emergence in New York, only 12,000 people lived in the 3,000 dwellings. Today, the World Trade Center, alone, houses at least ten times as many.

OBJECTIVE:

All three games are strictly time-killers when there are just too few people hangin' around to play Punch, Slap, or Stickball.

EQUIPMENT:

1 stoop
1 spaldeen
1 street light (for Nightball) and darkness

RULES:

Stoopball

The fielder gets the feeling of playing solitaire, though two people compete. The person in the field is the pitcher, the batter, and the catcher all-in-one (while his opponent sits on the sidewalk, bored).

Generally whoever is first up stands by the curb and hurls the ball against the stoop in the hope of catching the return without a bounce, thus scoring ten points. Less adept players just hope for a return. If the ball bounces once before the catch is made, five points are gained.

Any high-flying ball, caught off the edge of the step, is worth fifty or 100 points. The point scale is decided before the game begins (or after the fight). If the ball bounces more than once, or misses the stoop altogether, the player forfeits his turn to his friend who patiently waits and prays that his opponent will not reach the winning 1,000 points.

The games alternate between each player until one of them reaches the mark.

"When I was a small boy we lived at 120th Street and Mt. Morris Park, a neighborhood of brownstone stoop houses. Our favorite game was to stand just off the sidewalk and throw a golf ball at the steps. Each one that was caught counted "one." If the ball hit the leading edge of the step and was caught by the player, it counted "ten."

Yours sincerely,

Richard Rodgers

Richard Rodgers

One slight variation is *Stoop Baseball*, or Off the Wall. The batter throws the ball against the stoop, curb, or wall, and the other player, relinquishing his has-been status, fields the ball. Every bounce before the fielder retrieves the ball counts as a base hit, three bounces is a triple. But if the ball misses the stoop, or is caught on the fly, it's an out. Like Baseball, there are nine innings to the game, but there are no balls or strikes.

Curbball

As in Stoopball, two players and a ball constitute the requisites for the game. The batter stands two or three feet from the curb, winds up, and flings the ball against the curb. The ball soars through the air, into the street, where the fielder hurries to reach the ball. Doubles, singles, etc., are determined by the zone in which the ball bounces (see diagram). If the ball never reaches or leaves the curb, or if it is caught on a fly, the batter is out. Two outs, and the side retires. Other than the zoning system and the number of outs, the game follows the Baseball format.

Diagram:

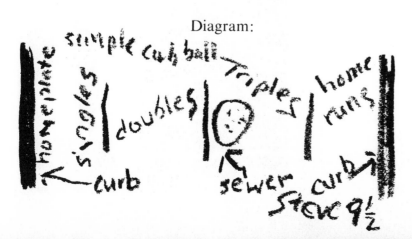

Nightball

Once the sun sets, and the "babies" are in the house, the big kids get going. The gas lamps on Beacon Hill in Boston provided the first lights, and the game has improved with technology from the incandescent to sodium vapor lamps being used in many cities today.

One or more fielders stand around the street light, while the batter, directly underneath the lamp, throws the ball as high as he can into the dark night. None of the fielders can see the ball as it journeys up past the light. Not until it descends from the darkness into the lighted area around the street light, can the players position themselves for the catch. More often than not, by the time they see it whizzing down in an unexpected place, it's too late. Until the ball is caught, though, every bounce is a base hit. A ball caught on a fly is an out. Two outs and the batter steps down. The scoring follows the lines of Stoopball (except that for every fly ball caught by a fielder there are at least three or four that land on his head, in which case the scoring is different).

Roofing

Roofing only requires a roof. Wherever there are large private homes with garages, Roofing is bound to be a part of the recreational scene. (In Michigan, particularly in the 40s and 50s, the game was called Iny-i-over.)

Two players stand, one to each side of a two-sided roof, so that neither can see the other or the ball coming over. In fact, the only warning before the ball actually appears is the call of "iny-i-over" from the person throwing the ball.

With a rapid increase in population, the more compact, one sided roof has become more prevalent. The pitcher throws the ball onto the roof, while the catcher stands close to the building in a position that blocks his view of the roof. The ball comes rolling down and off the roof, leaving little time for catching preparation. The catcher doesn't know where the ball will be falling until it hits the ground.

In actuality, Roofing is Nightball during the day and the rules of Nightball likewise apply.

Skelly

ORIGIN:

It is difficult to pinpoint the birth of Skelly, though the game relies heavily on a lazy man's approach to Hopscotch. Basically, bottle caps instead of feet hop through a series of numbered boxes chalked or painted on the street. Perhaps the word Skelly comes from "skeeter," a type of bug that whizzes across lakes and swamps as do the bottle caps on the pavement.

The game is played in most urban areas -- New Bedford, Boston, Atlanta, San Diego, Portland, and Tampa, to name a few. Without dispute, however, the Skelly capital of the world is Brooklyn, New York. If a player is from Brooklyn, for him, that is equivalent to the whole world.

The only prerequisites for the game are asphalt streets and bottle caps. After cobblestones replaced the dirt road in the early 19th century, it was only a few years before the first asphalt road was laid in this country in the spring of 1874 on I Street N.W., in Washington, D.C.

The other key element in the game, the bottle cap (Crown Cork and Seal) was born 17 years later. The proud father, William Painter, a machine shop foreman from Maryland, patented his brain child. He successfully succeeded in capping the 1,500 others who had made attempts at such an invention dating as far back as Ancient Egypt. On the 23rd birthday of his "crowns" (or caps), Coca-Cola introduced the design into its bottling plant, and the crown cap was well on its way to stardom. (It was a fruitful venture; the family of caps has grown to 330 million gross annually.)

The Skelly player need not fear for shortages -- there are miles of asphalt and plenty of caps around, though in some concerned areas, checkers have been substituted for bottle caps.

Though a specific date cannot be affixed to the first Skelly game, obviously it had to follow the invention of the cap and the application of asphalt to roads, since skimming caps across cobblestone or dirt roads was highly unlikely. The intersection of these two innovations puts the date for the beginning of Skelly somewhere at the turn of the 20th century.

EQUIPMENT:

Chalk to draw Skelly board

Bottle caps -- Rip out inner cork with a fork, melt crayon or candle wax into the cap to give it weight. Rub down the top into a smooth surface, and the cap is ready for action.

OBJECTIVE:

To hit the bottle cap through a series of numbered boxes until the center and luckiest box, number thirteen, is reached.

RULES:

First the diagram is laid out on the street neatly (see Diagram). Then each player, in turn, places his bottle cap (after it's been washed and polished) on the starting line and prepares the game strategy. (There actually is none, one must have faith.)

The method of locomotion for the bottle cap is rudimentary finger flicking. One neat flick of the forefinger propels the upside-down bottle cap across the asphalt to reach the desired target, which at the start is box 1. If the first flicker scuttles his Skelly cap into box 1, he goes again, shooting for number 2. Should success continue, the numerical ladder is climbed. Each time, the cap must be shot from any point within the box of the previous successful shot until 13 is reached, thus crowning the cap with the title "killer."

Should the player miss, he forfeits his turn to the next player who tries to follow, without failure, in his footsteps. When his turn next comes around, each player begins where he left off.

The major pitfall of the game is Skelly's Zone, the unnumbered space surrounding lucky 13. It's a bit like Monopoly—one bad chance, and you go back to Go without collecting the $200. If the cap goes astray and lands in this paved wasteland, it's back to the starting line, no matter what number you've reached. You are allowed to hit other players in your path, but such offensive strategy increases the risk of entering Skelly's Zone.

SCORING:

Once box 13 is reached, the process is reversed and every player shoots the numbers in descending order until reaching box 1. The first to make a complete cycle is the winner. Often the game is played well into the night, so it's impossible to see each other or the Skelly Board, making scoring a test of wills, eyesight, and chills.

DIAGRAM:

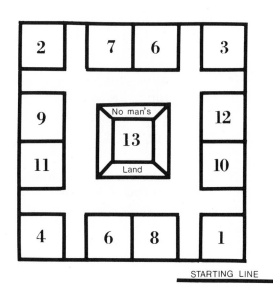

| 2 | 7 | 6 | 3 |

9	No man's	12
	13	
11	Land	10

| 4 | 6 | 8 | 1 |

STARTING LINE

Territory-Land

ORIGIN:

This knife game is tame when compared with Stretch. It was very popular during the first fifty years of the twentieth century but has been on the decline -- particularly in cities where dirt has succumbed to cement and asphalt. However, it is still easy to find a roughneck wearing a mohair sweater, clumping around with a knife stuck in his boot. He approaches his friends asking in a pre-pubic basso groan, "Wanna play Land, man?"

EQUIPMENT:

A plot of dirt
1 Jackknife

OBJECTIVE:

Each player tries to reduce his opponent's territory by either gaining his opponent's land or regaining his own.

RULES:

A square or circle eight inches in diameter is drawn in the dirt. A terrific tool used since Cro-Magnon man is the twig. Each player stands on one side of the dirt diagram. One player throws the knife into his opponent's territory or land. If the blade sticks in, at an angle no less than one thumb, the original dividing line is rubbed out, and the land is cut along new lines corresponding to the point and direction of the blade's entry. If Pythagoras were alive, he would certainly have a geometric fiasco.

After the angles and lines are agreed upon, the victimized owner (since this is an invasion of his territorial rights and privacy) chooses which piece of redivided land he wishes to keep. Then it is his turn to invade, tossing the knife into the piece of land left to his antagonist. The role of trespasser and trespassed is reversed, the old territorial lines are erased, and the land is carved up again, with the land holder who is attacked choosing the piece of land he must forfeit. Obviously, it will be the smaller piece. It is hard to be sympathetic to land owners, but as the surgery continues, someone's land diminishes until, sadly, he has no place to call his own. The one saving grace during this feudal war is that as one man's land shrinks, it becomes more and more difficult for the invading force to land his knife in the mini-acre. There is always a chance the tables or dirt will turn in the final gerrymandered land. Politicians should consider the import of this game in a child's education. In the end, if one cannot fit the heel of his shoe into his shrunken land, it is the end.

VARIATIONS:

Each player stands in his plot of land and follows the same rules and procedures as in Territory until there is so little room to stand on that the only place the knife can go is into his feet. The follow-through of this confrontation is a choice each individual must make for himself. Land development prospects are obviously poor. No one wants his plot, his final standing ground, to be his final resting place. Safe advice -- while there's still time, get out.

DIAGRAM

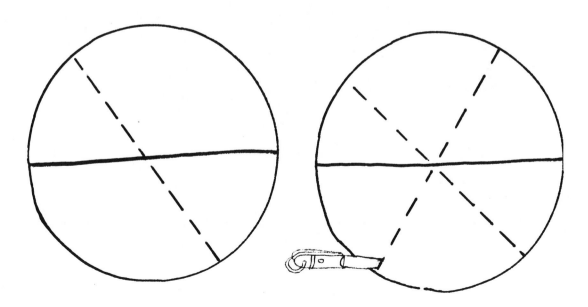

Keep *Away*

ORIGIN:

The spirit of Keep Away has been with man for thousands of years, though there is no formal record of the game before the 18th century. It was a popular pastime of the Russians, Australians, American Indians, and Italians in the early 1800s and 1900s. Perhaps as the melting pot melted, the game soaked its way into the national bloodstream of the United States. The game is played in all fifty states, and is second in popularity only to Cards, Candy, and Television.

EQUIPMENT:

1 basketball, volleyball (or piece of clothing)

OBJECTIVE:

For one team to keep the ball in motion without losing it to the other team.

RULES:

Any number can play this game, but even numbers work better in a team situation. The two teams must find a clearly definable way to distinguish themselves from one another. Very often it is the "skins" against the "shirts" (which in some parts of the country limits the game to warm weather and boys).

Everyone spreads around the street in pairs, one member of each team making up a pair. The ball is tossed into the center among the players. The team that gets the ball first passes it from one teammate to another, trying to keep it away from the opposing team members.

SCORING:

The first way to score is when each successful pass between team members counts one point. The team to reach twenty-one points first, wins.

The other method is a bit more complicated. During the game, each member passing the ball counts off a number, starting with one and consecutively increasing with each pass. If the ball is intercepted, the new holders of the ball start at number one. The game is played within a specific time limit. When the ball is returned to a team, the team continues the count from where it was left off. The team with the greatest number of passes within the set time limit wins.

VARIATIONS:

Saluggi

There is a resemblance to Monkey in the Middle in this game of "possession is nine-tenths of the law." It is mostly played during the school lunch hour. While everyone is anxiously waiting to return for the afternoon session, one victim is robbed of a hat or scarf, jacket or shoe. Cry babies are targets for this frolic, where one kid's possession is thrown around, hand-to-hand, by everyone. Unlike Keep Away, it's one poor soul against the crowd. All the other principles of the game remain until the principal arrives.

Hockey

This is Keep Away with a change of equipment. The hockey stick is substituted for the hands and a puck for the ball. In hands armed with weaponry, the players often overexert their confidence, and the result is assault and battery.

Frisbee®

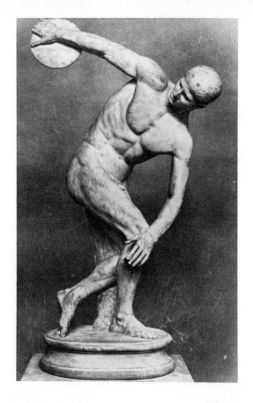

ORIGIN:

The strong resemblance between the Greek sculpture, *Discobolus,* by Myron and the modern Frisbee suggests that discus throwing has been around since the time of the ancient Greeks. The Official Frisbee Handbook offers another theory: Elihu Frisbee, in 1827, an undergraduate at Yale, "rebelled against compulsory chapel and heaved the collection plate across the campus quad." Another theory infers that the youngsters flinging pie tins among themselves gave the game its surname from the tins which came from the obsolete Frisbie Bakery of Bridgeport, Connecticut.

Whatever story one wishes to believe, no one can dispute the existence of Fred Morrison of Los Angeles, who approached the Wham-O Manufacturing Company with the idea of converting the discus, the collection plates, and pie tins, into a plastic flying saucer. Wham-O's Pluto Platter eventually evolved into the Frisbee. The craze swept the country; there are eight different models of Frisbee, 100 collegiate teams compete (Yale, Rutgers, Stanford, Princeton heading the list), over 600 cities participate in Junior Frisbee Tournaments and an IFA (International Frisbee Association with over 67,000 members) has been formed—in less than twenty-five years of its modern history.

RULES:

The wonderful thing about Frisbee is that there are no formal rules to the game. It is a free-form sport left to the creativity of the players. Perhaps this explains the game's popularity throughout the country, particularly among the young. There are basic games which are common -- the catch between two or more people—and by adding a touch of structure—Basketball, Football, Dodgeball, Golf, Saluggi, etc. The purposes of frisbeeing are limitless, be it shooting targets, meeting men or women at the park, gymnastic catches, or the thrill of watching the saucer soar through the air.

In the years to come, the IFA plans to coordinate the colleges into four regions as part of large national intramural sport. On the Junior level, over 1,200,000 kids, fifteen years and under, participate in the national tournament across the country.

Frisbee is one of the few games to have a police record. It was reported that several college students in Gambier, Ohio, were arrested for playing Frisbee in the streets during their spring session.

OFFICIAL PROFICIENCY RATING SYSTEM:

AMATEUR:

TEST AREA

A six-foot diameter circle should be drawn on the ground. Measuring from the center of the circle, at 15 yards distance, a "foul line" is drawn on the ground. The candidate must deliver his flights from behind the "foul line".

CONDITIONS AND

CATCHER WITHIN CIRCLE — 15 YDS. — FOUL LINE — POSITION OF CANDIDATE — 6'

The catcher is free to move anywhere within the six-foot diameter circle but is prohibited from stepping outside of it during the accuracy test. The candidate may elect to take any or all of the proficiency test within the 30-minute maximum time period allowed in each 24-hour day.

ACCURACY REQUIREMENTS

Each group of the following flights must be completed consecutively with no misses to the catcher, with the method of delivery the candidate's choice. If the flight is properly executed, and the catcher fails, it will be judged to be a completed flight.

The candidate may schedule the following seven flight groups in any order he wishes.

GROUP 1—Two Straight Flights

GROUP 2—One Right-Curve Flight

GROUP 3—One Left-Curve Flight

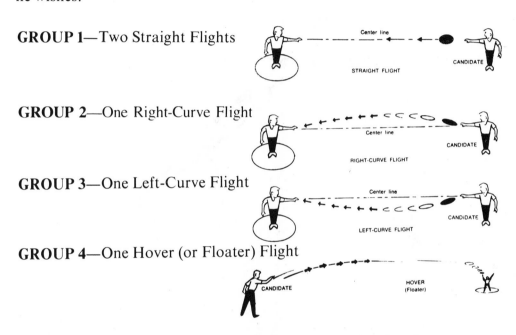

GROUP 4—One Hover (or Floater) Flight

GROUP 5—One Skip Flight (to be executed on any hard surface)

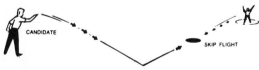

GROUP 6—Distance Flight whereby the candidate must obtain an average distance, in four flights, two up-wind and two down-wind, of not less than 20 yards.

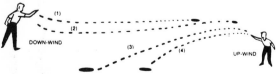

GROUP 7—Repeat any two of the above Groups 1 through 5 using opposite method of delivery, i.e. if backhand was used, throw underhand.

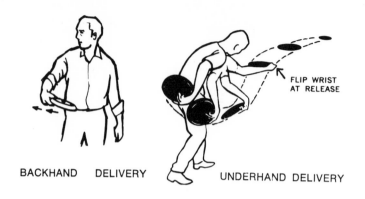

BACKHAND   DELIVERY   UNDERHAND DELIVERY

FLIP WRIST
AT RELEASE

CATCHING REQUIREMENTS

The candidate must be capable of catching two consecutive flights of any type using only the right hand, and two consecutive flights of any type using only the left hand, thrown from a distance of 15 to 20 yards. Note: These catches should be done consecutively; however, consideration will be allowed if the flights are not properly executed.

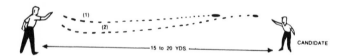

CANDIDATE

15 to 20 YDS.

Upon successful completion of the entire Amateur Proficiency Test, which is to be attested to by the judges on the candidate's proficiency rating card, the card and certification fee of $2 is sent to IFA headquarters for official sanction. The member will then receive certification as a FRISBEE Amateur and be issued a new membership card, expert proficiency rating card and special certificate.

Official Rules of Ultimate Frisbee (1971-72)

Presented by Columbia High School, Maplewood, New Jersey.

Ultimate Frisbee is a fast moving, competitive game played by two seven man teams.

PLAYING FIELD

The playing field may have any surface whatsoever, including grass, asphalt, sand, snow or the wood of a gymnasium floor. The two goal lines must be parallel. The main playing field for the official Ultimate Frisbee game is 60 yards by 40 yards with unlimited end zones.

If a pass is completed outside the lateral boundary it is considered incomplete and the team not in possession is given the Frisbee. In order to be considered in bounds, a player must land with both feet touching inside the boundary line. Should the Frisbee be thrown so that it leaves the lateral boundary it is returned to play on the main playing field at the point where it went out of the lateral boundary.

TIME

A game of Ultimate Frisbee lasts for 48 minutes of playing time divided into two 24 minute halfs. Half-time lasts for ten minutes and then the second half commences with a Throw-off by the team which received the opening Throw-off. The clock starts after every Throw-off and when the Frisbee is taken into play from out of bounds. The clock is stopped after every goal, for an injury, when a Frisbee goes out of bounds, when a time out is called, and at the end of the first half.

In the event of a tie at the end of regulation time, the team in possession receives a Throw-off from the opposing team starting a five minute overtime. If there is no victor at the end of the overtime, overtimes are continued until the tie is broken at the end of an overtime.

Each team is permitted three time-outs a half, each time-out lasting up to two minutes. In order to call a time-out, the team calling one must be in possession of the Frisbee.

OBJECT:

The object of the game is to gain points by scoring goals. The team with the most points at the end of the game is declared the winner. A goal is scored when a player on the field successfully passes the Frisbee to another player on the same team standing on the opposite side of the goal line which that team is currently attacking.

THROW-OFF

Play begins with the Throw-off. The captains of the two teams determine, by the flip of a coin which team will elect to throw or receive; the other team chooses which goal they will defend at the start. All players must stand on their own goal line until the Frisbee is released. One player designated by the captain of the team which is throwing off, throws the Frisbee toward the opposite end of the field. As soon as he releases the Frisbee all players may leave their positions on the goal lines. No player on the team throwing may handle the Frisbee until it has been touched by a member of the receiving team. That latter team now may do one of two things with the Frisbee which is flying toward them: a) catch it, or b) allow it to fall to the ground without touching it. If a member of the receiving team successfully catches the Frisbee thrown, that player has possession where it is caught, and if it is allowed to fall untouched to the ground the receiving team has possession where it lands and stops. If any member of the receiving team unsuccessfully attempts to catch the Frisbee thrown, or if the Frisbee comes in contact with any part of the body or clothing of any player on the receiving team and then falls to the ground, the team having thrown gains possession of the Frisbee where it lands and stops. Play continues immediately upon either team establishing possession of the Frisbee after the Throw-off.

THE PLAY

The team which has possession of the Frisbee must attempt to move the Frisbee downfield into position so that they may score a goal by passing the Frisbee over the goal line. *The Frisbee may be moved in only one way: it must be thrown. No player may walk, run or take any steps while in possession of the Frisbee during playing time.* The momentum of the receiver, however, must be taken under consideration. Should a player take steps obviously not required

*Ryan
and Tatum
O'Neal*

before stopping, he must return to the point where he gained possession and throw the Frisbee from there. A player may propel the Frisbee in any way he wishes, using one or both hands. If the Frisbee touches the ground, a tree, a wall or any object other than the body or clothing of another player, the Frisbee falls into possession of the team that did not last have possession. In case of a rolling or sliding Frisbee, the Frisbee may be stopped by any player, but may not be advanced in any direction.

As change in possession of the Frisbee occurs, any member of the team gaining the Frisbee may take possession of it. *The Frisbee may never be handed from player to player.* In order for the Frisbee to go from the possession of one player to that of another, the Frisbee must at some time be in the air and touching no solid object. The Frisbee may not be wrenched from the grasp of an opposing player, or knocked from his hand.

Members of the team which is not in possession of the Frisbee may gain possession in any of three ways: a) a player may catch the Frisbee thrown by a member of the opposite team and gain possession immediately where he catches it; b) a player may strike the Frisbee while in flight with his hand or any part of his body causing it to fall to the ground, gaining possession of the Frisbee where it falls and stops; c) a team gains possession of the Frisbee where it falls and stops whenever a member of the opposing team throws the Frisbee and it is not successfully caught by another member of the throwing team. Therefore, members of the team not in possession of the Frisbee gain possession whenever the offensive team does not successfully complete a pass from one member to another member of their team.

While no player may run with the Frisbee, the player in possession may pivot on either foot, as in basketball. Any *single* player on the opposing team may "guard" a player in possession of the Frisbee and attempt to block his throw (although he may not knock the Frisbee out of the opponent's hand). The guarding player may not touch the body or clothing of the player whom he is guarding, nor may he grasp the Frisbee until it has left the hand of the man attempting to throw. If he does do so the player throwing regains possession at the same spot.

END ZONES

Anytime possession of the Frisbee changes from one team to the other and in the course of doing so crosses either goal line, the team gaining possession may choose to begin play at the goal line. A player may carry the Frisbee up to the playing field provided that he approach the goal line directly perpendicular to it. Should a team gain possession in the end zone which it is attacking, the Frisbee must be returned to the goal line of that end zone before play may be continued.

FOULS

No player may strike the body of any other player in an attempt to block a throw or a catch. Players must expect a certain amount of body contact when two or more jump up for a high throw. A player throwing the Frisbee is fouled when there is physical contact between himself and a member of the opposing team sufficient to deter the path of travel of the throw.

A player attempting to receive a throw is fouled by any flagrant physical action by an opponent (pushing, clipping, holding, kicking, submarining, etc.) which is sufficient to arouse the ire of the player fouled.

In the event of a foul, the player fouled gains possession of the Frisbee at the point of infraction. Should the foul occur in the end zone, the player fouled gains possession of the Frisbee at the goal line. The call of a foul may be declined by the team against which the foul was committed if they so desire (i.e. the pass is completed anyway).

SCORING

Play continues until a goal is scored. As soon as a goal is scored the team having scored the goal throws off to the other team on the signal of the referee or the captain of the receiving team. Each time a goal is scored the teams switch the direction of their attack and defend the goal which they have just finished attacking. A team is awarded one point for each goal legally scored, and there is no other way to gain points.

SUBSTITUTIONS

Substitutions can be made in only three circumstances: a) after a goal is scored before the next Throw-off; b) to replace an injured player; c) at halftime. Substitutions cannot be made during a timeout.

GROUND RULES

Before the opening Throw-off, the captains of the two teams may agree on any additional ground rules necessary. Although the official rules are stated, these rules may be adapted to the size of the teams and the physical limitations of the field.

A NOTE ON TEAM SIZE & FIELD SIZE

While the CHS Varsity Frisbee team, developers of Ultimate Frisbee, state that 7 players is the official number for each team, this sport can be played with as many as 20 or 30 for each team, if a large enough field is available. Naturally, the skills needed in the game will diminish as the group gets too large.

Ultimate Frisbee can be played without any lateral boundaries, as it was played originally, however, it is best to choose a field with natural boundaries such as trees, a river or a hill.

ONE HAND ULTIMATE

As proficiency with Ultimate Frisbee increases, a "one-hand only" form of the game can be tried. In this variation the Frisbee may be caught cleanly in one hand only. If two hands are used or if the player's body is employed to "trap" the Frisbee in any way, possession of the Frisbee is forfeit to the opposing team. The restriction applies to both teams, but a defending player may still use both hands or any part of his body to knock down the Frisbee in flight.

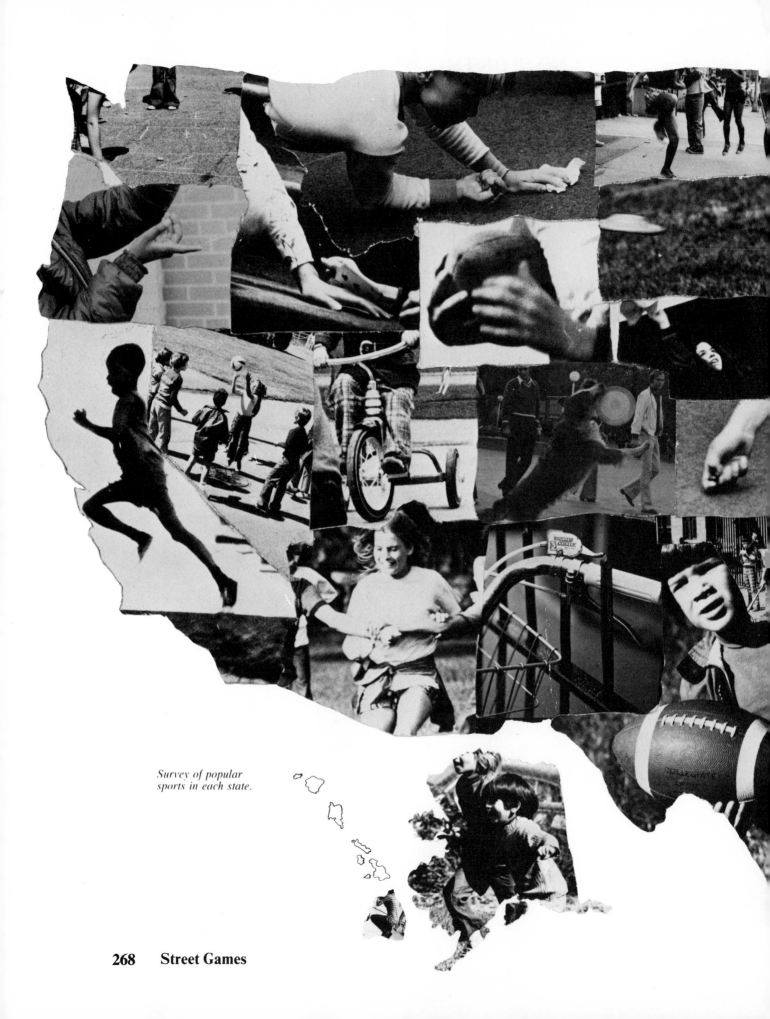

Survey of popular sports in each state.

Game
Map USA

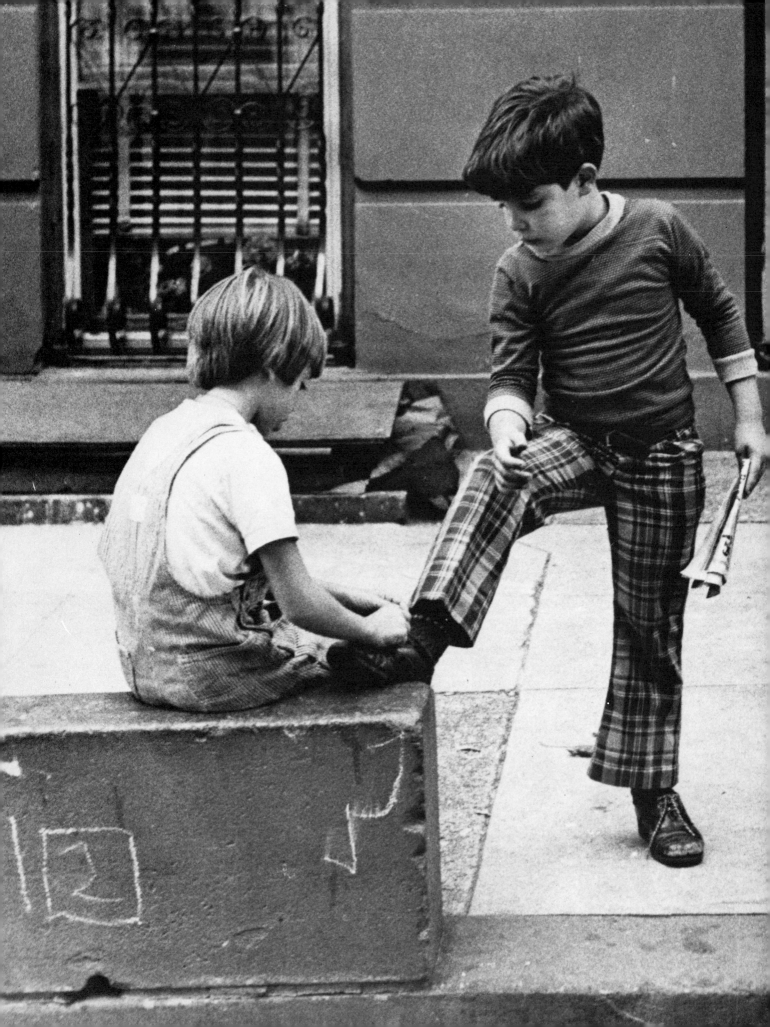

Overtime

Intricate Street Games for Saigon's Children

By DAVID K. SHIPLER
Special to The New York Times

SAIGON, South Vietnam, Sept. 14—Eight-year-old Dao Chich, whose nickname means "Burglar," holds a sandal up to one eye and squints seriously along the sole, taking careful aim at a small cluster of rubber bands that he and his two opponents have put on the sidewalk about 30 feet away.

With a sudden snap of his wrist, he sends the sandal skimming just above the pavement, sliding precisely into the little stack of rubber bands and spraying them across the concrete. Dao Chich has won again. He scampers down the sidewalk, picks up the rubber bands and stuffs them into his pocket.

Saigon is a city of street games. Along the broad boulevards, in the quiet side streets, deep among the labyrinths of lanes and alleys that lace the city, children play with what they have, making ingenious games of the simplest ingredients: sandals and rubber bands, cans and bottle caps, chopsticks and coins, corncobs and sticks, marbles and stones, broken bits of brick.

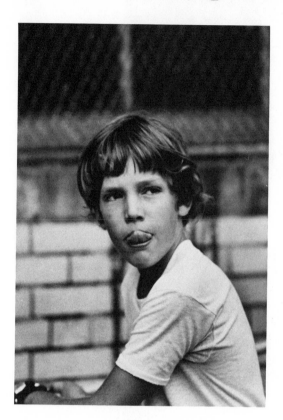

Super Sun

By JAMES T. WOOT
Special to The New York Ti

PHILADELPHIA, Oct Today, for the secon in three weeks, th of people jammed center of this old celebrate — well brate whatever s fancy.

It was Super annual event the Benjamin F way is conver boulevard to and which is enthusiasts biggest block

Amateur Athletes Rise To Olympian Heights Here

Korvettes Street G

By ROBERT CARROLL

You knew it wasn't the Olympics when beefy, T-shirted beer salesman Dick Ryan trotted up carrying a torch fashioned from an empty flashlight case and lit the can of Sterno on top of the flag-draped garbage can.

Cheers Philadelphians

N.Y.'s 'Asphalt Olympics': Old Games Remade

By GOLDMAN

'Asphalt Olympics' Give City Games New Glow

ers where ways.

kind of
driv:

Spaldeen Olympiad

By MICHAEL T. KAUFMAN

With the ceremonial lighting of an "eternal garbage can" by a 260-pound torchbearer who ran all the way around the corner of City Hall yesterday, the city's Olympiad of street games was officially proclaimed.

The games, open to all New Yorkers 16 years of age and older who register with the Department of Recreation, will be held at 18 locations in the five boroughs.

Games Entry Blank

☐ **STICKBALL (5 players & 1 alternate)**
☐ **STOOPBALL (3 players & 1 alternate)**
☐ **JOHNNY-ON-THE-PONY (5 players & 1 alternate)**
☐ **CHINESE HANDBALL (Individual)**
☐ **BOXBALL (Individual)**
☐ **PUNCHBALL (Girls) (5 players & 1 alternate)**

You can enter only one team and one individual event.
Open to those 16 and older, boys and girls.
Official entry forms must be filled out prior to play

1. Did play touch football, base runner, basketball
baseball

2. I enjoyed the competitive spirit
and inflicting pain

3. Same as 1

LARRY Nelker

1. Street football @ Stick
" hockey @ SPUD
skate board 5 Bikes

2. Like | Dislike
winning | cars
ob ladies
Girls in the game

3. street football
Wiffel Ball.

Laura Walden

1. baseball, jumprope, kickball
football, bike riding, spud,
quek dodge, sled riding

2. I use to be on the losing
team, always went through
paddlewheel, fell off track and
ripped my pants and knees.
liked being with friends.

3. vindictive neighbor game
takes balls, watch the lawn

Robent Lowe
1. Street Hockey, touch Football, have played.

2. Falling, Getting hit in the Crotch with a pock.

3. touch football, Street hockey, Kickball,

Scott Fechbach

1) Bike Riding }- present
   Sledding

   sledding
   cops + robbers
   catch with baseball   } Past
   skateboarding in
   the sewers

2) I enjoy bike riding for the exercise
   sledding for the accidents.

3) Bike riding, pulling wagon

Tim Lotz
1. Step ball, keepaway,
   sledding, bicycling, tag

2. Like them all

   because no rules

3. kickball

MaryBethDembeck

Played in past:
J.P.U.D., kick ball, football, rode bike, hide n' seek, kick the can
hop scotch, rollar skate, skate board, jump rope, spot light
& army, hoola hoop

People always cheated and one guy always got
hurt and would cry and go home, this would ruin
the game making the teams uneven.
   I liked football the best.

3. badmitton in the back yard, kick the can, ride bikes,
army

1.) Have played: hopscotch, jump rope; red line;   Elizabeth Pipkin
    roller skate; hand ball; kick ball;   None done now;
    soccer; yelled at cars; ring doorbells   All in past.
    spud; truth or dare; dodge; sledriding.

2.) The reason i liked all these game were because they were played
with everyone - never mattered how old you were - it was
like one group. Never liked the bad end of the deal -
   EX) holding the jump-rope end.

3.) baseball; soccer; football; mini-bike riding;

Mary Lucian Gogarty

1. SPUD
   Kick ball
   Dodge
   Jump rope
   hop schoch
   rollar skate)
   skate board
   tag (freeze)
   hockey
   hide i seek
   base runners
   * make the truck drivers blow their horns
   red light
   mother may i?

2. i was one of the oldest in the
   neighborhood i couldn't stand
   all the little kids always butting in.
   i liked most of the game or i
   wouldn't have played

3. bike riding
   Frisbee
   rollar skate

Becky

1. rode tricycle, played hopscotch, all in past
   and Dodge, played SPUD, Hide + Seek, jump rope *

2. Didn't like Greek Dodge that much if I played
   with people who were better than me (for obvious
   reasons).
      Loved jump rope because everyone took
   equal turns and made up verses to it. It was fun!

3. Baseball, football, smoke dope (believe it or not -- in public)

① Four Squares, Hop Skotch, Skate Board, Base Runners, Football, Sledding -- Past

② ~~Like~~ - ~~Four s~~ Like - to be with friends in the neighborhood - to be apart
   Dislike - didn't have fun with neighbors though

③ Tennis, Flash-light Tag.   Michele Josselyn

CAROL McPHEE

PAST
{
GREEK DODGE -
KICK THE CAN
HOP SCOTCH
S.P.U.D.
RIDE BIKE
ROLLAR SKATE
KICK BALL
JUMP ROPE
}

They were fun because everygame we played had
a large group of people. But ... sometimes
it was bad because there were bad sports
and it resulted in fights.
Army
Bike riding
Catch

Mike 16

1.) Build a Dam in the gutter   Played

2.) Likes   DISLIKES
you can float your boat   Got pretty Dirty
                             DAM BREAKS
3.) Too young   Getting run over by car or Boat

①
1 roller skate
2. jump rope
3. hopstoch
4. skateboards
5 Kick the Can
6 I spy
7. Dodge
8. KickBall
9. Football ↙59
10. Softball
11. Spud

② Roller skate - everytime when I
fell my skates would fall off & I'd
Rate putting them back on

I Spy - I loved that game because
we played at night & tried to
hide from the other team. And I
liked to hide with the boys in
my alley.
Football - I liked getting tackled
from the guys.
③ my neighbors play: Kick Ball
Baseball, hopsotch, jump rope
    Kathy Daly

Larry Bartour.

1. road my bike in the street

2. You can get killed

3. like riding

1. Cops Robbers, flashligt Tag : just Rumbles, Snowballs
2. ~~too~~ Steidsleighs
    2. play Cops + Robbers onbikes I fell into a rose
bush
3. They don't

Mitsuro Iguisa

1) tag, soccer, wiffle ball, throwing snowballs, and lacross
   - these were the games I played in the past

2) These games were fun especially throwing snowballs, also its fun to try to hill the other person. But the street is a little rough on your knees and your behind.

3) ~~one fear~~ sled riding, tag, and climbing trees,

Dea Roubenstine

Sled riding /played
1. Bike riding /played

2 Liked - freedom a control while on bike
   Sled riding - dislike the feeling of loss of control

3 Bike riding, Soccer

HAVE PLAYED

1) rode bikes, pitched pennys, played ball, stick, roller skated hide o seek between the cars.

2) hated having a car break up a game or getting hit by a car, losing all my pennies.

CAROL Miller

3) none - rural neighborhood.

Kick Ball
Soft Ball
Hop Scoth
Skeleton
Hide an' seek

Biking 3 present

Skeleton always scared me for the simple
reason that it was played in the dark;
also the idea of being chase by
some thing evil terrified me. The same
with Hide and seek, for some
strange reason every time I hid I
adimaticly had to go to the bathroom.

Pal Gaffney

I don't know

UNICEF greeting cards: Street Games Around the World

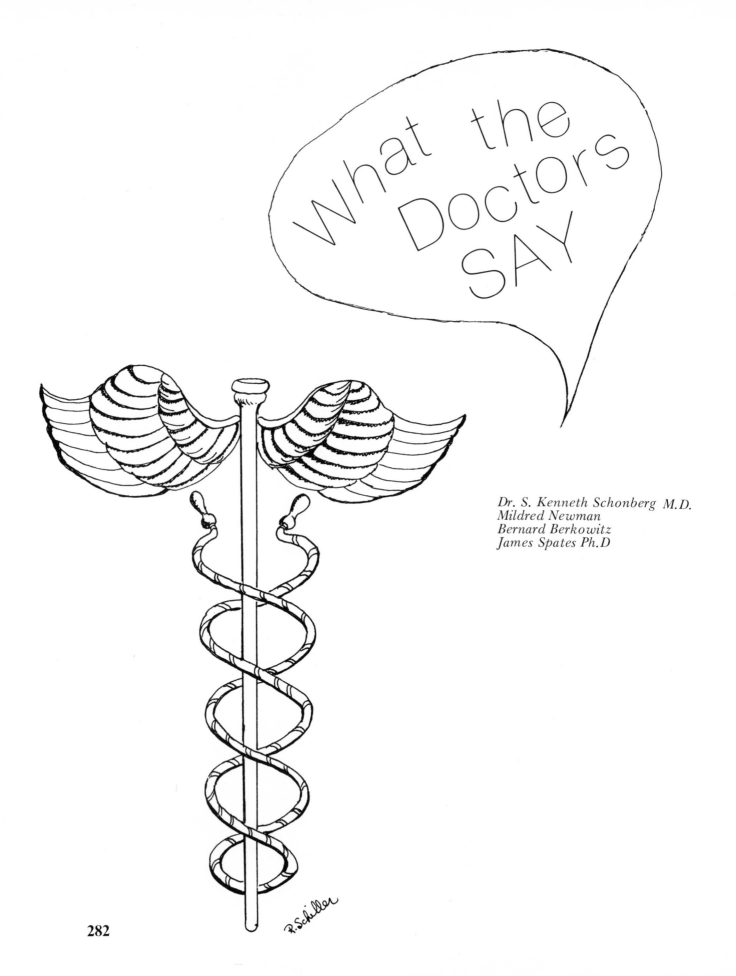

What the Doctors SAY

Dr. S. Kenneth Schonberg M.D.
Mildred Newman
Bernard Berkowitz
James Spates Ph.D

R. Schiller

282

Medical Overview

S. Kenneth Schonberg, M.D.
Attending in Pediatrics
Montefiore Hospital and Medical Center
Albert Einstein College of Medicine

The decision to partake in street games is not made out of desire for physical fitness, nor is the choice to avoid these activities made on a rational appraisal of the medical risks involved in participation. A pediatrician's counsel on these diversions is seldom sought or offered, and even the most organized of street hockey teams would regard with amusement the suggestion that certification of physical fitness be a prerequisite for team membership.

Although minor injuries must be numerous, injuries severe enough to require medical attention are relatively infrequent. Hence the "Medical Overview of Street Games" is not only made from above, but also from a great distance.

"School's Out—Drive Carefully" - and yet the warm long days of summer continue to take their toll on young athletes who have taken to the streets to play. "Pedestrian" accidents continue to be a leading cause of childhood death and injury. It is not possible to denote the proportion of these accidents attributable to street games; however if such data were available, the street game would probably emerge as the most dangerous youthful sport.

By comparison, other acute medical risks are of minor significance and usually involve fast moving young bodies challenging immovable objects. The vast majority of such injuries never come to the attention of the pediatrician. The youngster's choice of treatment for a minor injury would be concealment from both parent and physician, as a week of pain is often more desirable than a day of restricted activities.

Even those injuries which go beyond the child's ability to conceal and the parents' ability to treat may be falsely attributed to a more acceptable etiology than a street game. The street game injury seldom receives the combination of sympathy and admiration afforded skiing fractures or dueling scars. The more worldly youngster will skillfully invent a work related cause for his disability such as falling down at school or over-exertion in taking out the garbage. Nevertheless, some trauma clearly attributable to Johnny on the Pony, Street Hockey, and Tag Football does make its way to the pediatrician's office. Minor lacerations, loose front teeth, sprained ankles, wrists and fingers and an occasional fracture represent the majority of such cases.

Internal injuries, such as ruptured spleens and head trauma (concussions) are more commonly associated with organized juvenile sports but are also an infrequent complication of street games. As previously stated, the total number of such injuries requiring medical attention remains relatively small considering the large number of youngsters playing street games. If one were to eliminate the moving automobile from the discussion of acute medical risks, street games would not constitute a major health problem.

With the exception of those instances where a youngster sustains a permanent injury while at play, the relationship between early sports activity and adult disability is in most respects unclear. Little League baseball has imposed strict regulations on the duration and frequency that a youngster may pitch so as to minimize the risk of acute or chronic injury to the arm and elbow. The risks to the arm of the stickball pitcher are essentially the same with no limitation upon innings pitched or days of rest between games. Recent years have seen great emphasis placed on the development of better protective equipment and safer playing surfaces for organized football, and yet injuries to joints, in particular knees, continue to result in long term disability. One must assume that tag football played without safety equipment and often on the most dangerous of playing fields carries at least some of the long term risks. The number of adults who owe their chronic low back pain to indulging in Johnny on the Pony is a fertile field for, if not investigation, at least speculation. To keep this discussion in balance, one could speculate on the adult risks of obesity, cardiac insufficiency and exercise intolerance resultant from never having participated in street games.

Some mention of risks to non-participants must be made. These risks are well known to anyone who has failed to appreciate that their street had been converted into a stickball court, a street hockey rink, or tag football field. The frequency of injury to such intruders serves to preserve the sanctity of the playing field, as one seldom makes that mistake twice. Also deserving of special attention is the injuries to the body, clothing and, in particular, the motorist target during a game of "hydrant."

In summary, major medical complications of street games are infrequent considering the large numbers of youngsters involved in these activities. Many of the injuries which do occur are a result of the fact that street games are played in the street and could be eliminated if safe play areas were universally accessible. However, the behavioral consequences of relocation to areas designed and controlled by adults might constitute a treatment worse than the disease.

Psychological Overview

by Mildred Newman
& Bernard Berkowitz

From the point of view of psychology of the individual, what a child makes of a game largely determines what the game might do to or for him. But the child is not simply passively acted upon. What he gets out of his play experiences is strongly influenced by the attitudes he brings to them.

For example, some youngsters could have paranoid reactions in almost any game situation, if they brought that kind of personality and predisposition into the game to begin with. That does not make any of the games inherently paranoid.

By the same token, a test of strength could be no more than that for most participants, but the same game involving such a test could be used sadistically by some kids, masochistically by others and both sadistically and masochistically by still others. Thus, no game is inherently "good" or "bad," with the exception of Russian Roulette which is always *bad* no matter how you spin the cylinder.

The following are some of the possible outcomes of the experiences that (the listed) games conceivably could afford to different participants. Clearly the same game can have different effects, and the four categories below are not mutually exclusive.

I. Initiation Rites

These games could provide the basis for inclusion or exclusion from the group.

II. Competition

These games may be seen as tests or comparisons of relative strength, speed, skill, coordination, daring, courage, and at the extreme as possible sublimation of aggressive and murderous feelings.

III. Cooperation

These games can be seen as exercises or training in getting along with others; role training, mainly superordination and subordination, or the giving and taking of orders.

IV. Emotional Control

The stress here is to test frustration tolerance and to develop ability in this sphere.

Sociological Overview

by Dr. James Spates
Assistant Professor,
Hobart and William Smith Colleges,
Geneva, New York

The major emphasis in many modern cultures is the expectation that people must be "the best" at what they do and must find some recognizable means of demonstrating such "success". Thus the sociological concerns are the symbolic nature of street games on the normative and role levels. Street games can be categorized in three major classes; competitive, aggressive and acquisitional.

COMPETITIVE GAMES

Strictly speaking, almost all street games are competitive or variations on a competitive theme. The reason for this directly links to a major emphasis in American society: the demand that the individual be a winner, or alternatively, "on top", "number one", and by that gain a certain amount of high prestige (respect and admiration) and power (the ability to control the situation) which does not devolve on the loser. In general, the winner is expected to exhibit joy and release upon his victory ("Hooray!"), as well as a certain amount of pride ("I worked hard. I deserved to win."), self-effacement ("Ah, shucks, anybody could'a done it."), and magnaminity to his opponent ("He played a good game, but ..."). In contrast, the loser is expected to exhibit correspondingly opposite thoughts and actions: sadness and frustration upon defeat ("Damn it all anyway!"), and, depending on the severity of the loss, adequate amounts of shame ("I just didn't have it today."), self-servingness in the form of excuses ("If I'd only not slipped in the fourth inning ..."), and restrained anger at his opponent ("Just wait 'til next time!").

(A) One Winner, Many Losers. The best example of this variation of competitive street games is "King-of-the-Mountain." This is a very gratifying game from the winner's point-of-view, for he learns what it is like (however briefly is his tenure on top before being thrown off), to be an unequivocal success, to be unquestionably better than the entire competition. Simultaneously, he is likely to feel the admiration and envy of his peers (prestige) as well as his total mastery of their and his fate (power). However, there are important "problems" associated with the King role. On the one hand he is likely to experience the extremely precarious nature of his position, in that he must be continually fending off challenges to his authority. There is a limitation to just how much one can endure of this type of unceasing "pressure" in such a situation. On the other hand, being the sole victor, he is also likely to feel a certain, insurmountable, alienation from his peers, and the resultant loneliness of this: if there is none better than he, with whom can he commiserate, whom can he trust?

On the loser's side, not winning at King-of-the-Mountain is not as serious a situation as it may be in other competitive game variations, simply because one is not alone at losing. There are others who have lost as well, and with these "failures" the individual can commiserate. There are, of course, often gradations in the loser role: for example, that between those who quit trying entirely ("the sissies") and those who continue, though with no chance of success, to depose the King ("the regular Joes"). To the extent that such distinctions develop, more or less of the loser's mental and behavioral patterns can be expected to be in evidence. (Thus, a "regular joe" may say of a "sissie": "Well, maybe I didn't get to be King, but at least I didn't quit like that ..."). Whatever it's gradations, however, the loser role teaches those that play it what it feels like to be second best in competitive situations and strongly suggests that, in the future, one should do his utmost to keep from being in that category of lesser social favor.

(B) **Many Winners, One Loser.** Tag, Blindman's Bluff and Keep Away are often played by younger children. The key issue in winning at this variation is to be part of the group. As intimated in discussion of the King game, there is a certain amount of positive emotional sustenance provided by a group: if you lose, at least you're not the only one; if you win, you are, if not the sole winner, one of "the best."

In the many winners, one loser variation, the worst role, by far, is that of "it," particularly if you can't get "out of 'it'." In this latter possibility, the loser does not have even the minimal requisite qualities to be a member of the group. For all intents and purposes, this is the "loser of losers" role. Because they recognize the psychological consequences of being put in this social role, many players of this type of game accidentally "allow" the person who is "it" to get "out of 'it' " by catching them (hoping, of course, that when they are in a similar position, others will give them the same consideration). But even brief experiences of the helplessness that accrues to this loser role is enough to teach the individuals who have played it, as well as those that have merely observed its consequences, that one of the worst things that can happen to one in our society is to be completely without the skills necessary for membership in any group. The person in this position is a true outcast in the extreme case and an object of pity and derision in the lesser case: both very distressing possibilities. Participants in these games will do *almost anything* to get "out of 'it'."

(C) **One Team Winner, One Team Loser.** The basic principles of the one team winner, one team loser variety of competitive games are the same as the varieties already discussed. However, team games introduce an element of qualification on the winner or loser roles simultaneously, by eliminating the sole, isolated individual role. By combining efforts in a team, players diffuse responsibility and lower risks - there is no total loss or victory by one individual.

Despite the "compromise" of the team effort, however, all is not lost as far as individual recognition is concerned. If it were it is unlikely that in our "get ahead", "be the best" society, team gains would be as popular as they are. I am speaking of the specialized roles that develop within a team so that the game may be played. To take a specific example, the "tag football" team can be, in its most elaborate form, broken down into virtually all the specialized roles that can be found on any formalized football team: ends, tackles, guards, centers, quarterbacks, halfbacks, fullbacks, etc. In first playing this game each player is assigned one of these pre-designated roles and learns what he is to do within that position by playing it. As the game is played again and again, each player generally shifts to all positions, trying them all at least once, thereby gaining an understanding of what these roles feel like "from the inside." However, over time, there is a tendency for individual players to "lock themselves into" the specialized role that they are best at and to play that role continually. By so doing, people so "specialized" get a "reputation" among other players as being a "good end," a "good quarterback," a "good halfback," and the like. Consequently, as they play the roles more, they are expected to take on the social characteristics normally associated with the role: "Ends are fast as hell and have good hands." "Quarterbacks are smart." "Halfbacks are big, tough, dumb, and mean."

AGGRESSIVE GAMES

One of the means that is often useful in forging one's way to "the top" is the use of aggression, either physical or mental. However, in light of being "fair," most groups in American society frown on the overt use of aggressive tactics by one individual or group against another because it is realized that aggression is usually neither part of inherent skill at playing a legitimate role nor is it necessary in attaining the top positions. Yet, despite this overt repudiation, the possibility and temptation to use aggressive tactics remains in many social situations. It is difficult, if not impossible, for many of the people who aspire to these most rewarded positions to attain them. (There is, after all, only *one* President of the United States, and have only been thirty-eight in our history, despite the fact that probably millions of Americans have, at one time or another, however briefly, aspired to hold that position.) As a result of this social structural reality, all Americans, to some degree, have to learn to live with some amount of "failure" in many areas of life, if not all. Consequently, they have to learn to live with the resultant anxiety that develops in the struggle for the top positions as well as the actual frustration that accrues when it becomes clear that they cannot "make it." Such frustration, in itself, produces a tendency towards aggressive acts as a means of (1) venting the built-up tension and (2) gaining a certain amount of revenge on the objects of one's frustration (other human beings, either those who have directly frustrated us or their symbolic representatives in other people).

(A) **Overtly Aggressive Games.** Since overt aggression is in disfavor in our society-at-large, these games tend to be few in number and played on an individual-vs.-individual basis. The central idea that is expressed by these is this: in this specially sanctioned situation, the winner is licensed to physically attack his opponent without defensive retaliation. The basic roles are, in the classic sense, those of dominance and submission.

Actual examples of these games range all the way from the slapping of hands variation ("I get to slap your hands as hard as I want to, until I miss. Then, it's your turn."), to "flinch" ("I will pretend to hit you. If you move or blink when I do this -- i.e., 'flinch' -- I get to really hit you."), to the more sadistic "knuckles" ("We play a hand of cards. If I win the hand, I get to smash your knuckles with the edge of the deck of cards as hard as I want."). The ultimate winner -- the dominant role player -- in these varieties of overtly aggressive games is the player who wins the most "rounds" in the competition (he who makes the other fellow's hand the reddest in hand slapping; he who gets the most "hits" in "flinch," he who makes the other person's knuckles the bloodiest in "knuckles"). Lastly, in this group, there is the completely victorious "Give Up," or "Cry 'Uncle'." ("We wrestle -- fight, etc. -- The game is over when one of us so beats the other that the other completely "gives up" all pretense of winning and completely accepts the loser's role -- the submissive role -- without excuse.")

(B) **Covertly Aggressive Games.** Because overtly aggressive games can develop into sadistic routines and because they are not legitimized in adult roles under most circumstances, there is a greater tendency for most young people to "hide" their aggressive impulses within the rules of other games. Everyone playing these games is aware of and generally agrees on the legitimacy of such covert tactics. There is a dual social function in this: not only are the aggressive players thus protected from the censure of adults and their peers for being overtly, inexcusably aggressive, but covert aggression is the principal way aggression is utilized in the adult world in our society.

In playing King-of-the-Mountain, for example, the King is allowed on occasion to use excessive force on his challengers in order to keep them from attaining his vaunted position; in "Keep Away," the group can decide to keep the ball away from the loser forever if they have the skill to do so. But it is particularly in team games that the aggressive element is most legitimate and most covert. In running the bases of stickball, for example, the runner may hit, very hard, anyone in his way; similarly, the person trying to tag him out, may tag him extremely hard without causing any undue concern among the other players. In playing tag football, someone throwing a block at an opposing player can hit him much harder than is necessary to make an effective block and get away with it. Often, the entire aggressive act may be hidden from the view of other players and spectators because of the number of people involved in playing the game or the fact that the "action" of the game is elsewhere.

Of course, in adult life, most of what is physically aggressive in these street games must be translated into mental aggression. Despite this necessity, the street games provide all the central characteristics of such thought and behavioral patterns: they allow us to understand which aggressive acts are possible, who can be aggressive to whom, how the acts may be most effectively perpetrated and what it feels like to play the dominant role in such an exchange as well as the submissive one.

ACQUISITIONAL GAMES

In American society there are three main symbols which are recognized as being indicative of one's success in life, prestige, power, and wealth. In our discussion so far we have seen that the first two of these qualities are always a central issue in competitive and aggressive street games. The symbol of wealth, however, is almost always attached to specific material goods such as possessions and money. Both are seen as being indicative of "jobs well done." Obviously, in the games already dealt with there are no material rewards that are "taken home" as a result of playing the winners role. Consequently, it is not surprising that American children have developed a series of games where the chief normative emphasis is to win material goods (wealth) and the principal roles are "the possessor" and "the dispossessed." Examples of such games are legion: flipping coins, flipping cards, playing marbles, being just a few. The basic idea of these games is to put your skill and luck against an opponent with the objective being the acquisition of part of the opponent's collection that he has to put up as stake.

Obviously, all the elements of true gambling are in these games and players can learn the paramenters of this gambling role for many situations in later life -- ranging from actually "betting on the horses," to risking one's job possibilities on saying certain things in a job interview. More than this, however, is the feeling tone involved in the roles of possessor and dispossessed. He who wins and possesses learns that other people admire and often envy those who have "things" that they themselves do not have. Possession is a reward in itself. On the other hand, he who loses and is dispossessed learns that to have little in the way of the valued "things" means that little admiration will come to him from others. Worse, he may learn, in some situations, that not possessing may be a gateway to his subsequently being ridiculed ("You've only got *three* marbles?") or cast out of situations ("You can't play if you don't have any playing cards."). This, like other loser roles in the individual-vs.-individual situation is very difficult to bear psychologically. Hence, one of the basic ideas socialized in acquisitional games is that the accumulation of things is good; it is symbolic of one's success in the same way that the prestige and power of other street games is symbolic of success and is minimally required even for participation in many situations.

SUMMARY

Street games are not haphazard inventions concocted with the sole purpose of enjoyment. They certainly have such a pleasurable function, but they are developed for yet another, crucial purpose: as a means of practicing on their own (via self-socialization) and within their own context (the child's world) the ways of living that children, however subconsciously, know (via other means of socialization) will be important in adult life contexts within their social order.

GLOSSARY

Aggies:	Marbles, formerly agates.
Ball Tag:	Person is tagged-out with ball instead of hand.
Baste the Bear:	A variation of Monkey in the Middle except the person in the center of the circle, the Bear, chooses another, his Keeper, to join him in the center. Children forming the circle try to tag the Bear without being tagged by the Keeper.
Bowling:	In Marble-Rolling, the shot along the ground to hit the "aggie."
Butterfingers:	Picking up a stone in Hopscotch by putting one hand on the pavement for balance. Must be called before the game starts.
Butting in:	A major cause of fights.
Car:	The most annoying enemy in street play; also the code word (commonly screamed) when a moving vehicle approaches a moving player.
Catch Ball:	A variation of Monkey in the Middle, but the ball is passed around the circle rather than across the circle.
Chips:	A player, usually one materialistically inclined, will call "chips" on a ball or piece of sports equipment. This is usually the standard retail value of the piece of equipment. Whoever loses the ball must pay up, without any depreciation factor, though the ball may be twelve years (or more) old.
Cooties:	A "disease" given to disliked kids by saying "Cooties on you" and tagging them; conversely when an unpopular player joins a game a "Cooties shot" (an imaginary injection) is given to protect friends from the "disease."
Crab Soccer:	Soccer played by moving on all fours (face and stomach upward) rather than on two legs.
Cross-my-heart:	A deal sealed with an honorable swear. (Most often when double-dealing with a smile, the swearer makes his statement with his fingers crossed, well-hidden from view; *see* Fingers, Crossed.)
Cry Baby:	When one individual cries, to the embarrassment or against the wishes of another, he is declared a cry baby (though tears may be of valid cause).

Do-over:	Whenever the flight of ball is interrupted by a house, wall, passerby, or car, "Do-over" is shouted by the batter in the hope of another chance to swing. Even if the batter doesn't like his shot or the way the wind is blowing, he takes a chance at calling "Do-over," realizing he has little to lose.
Enders (first):	Job of holding jump rope; first ender is next person in line to jump rather than end.
Even-the-score:	Usually refers to hostile activity by two members of opposing teams after game has ended.
Fifty-two Pick-Up:	Initiation rite for new kid in town, requiring him to pick up fifty-two strewn playing cards.
Fingers, Crossed:	Invalidates sworn testimony or promise.
First:	Herald made by any individual anxious to be first in game.
Flies up:	A ball hit into the air. (In catching fly balls, the mind and body at early ages are relatively together; as age advances, the mind sees the fly and says, "Go get it," while the body replies, "Who me?")
For Fair:	As in the National Marbles Tournament, all marbles are returned to each player at the end of the game.
Foreplay:	The type of play at the beginning of a game such as Blind Man's Bluff.
For Keeps:	The winning player gets to keep all the marbles hit out of the ring.
Fudging:	(In unofficial play only.) Putting hand over the ring line during a shot.
Fungo:	The ball thrown in the air by the batter, in games in which batter acts also as pitcher, swinging or kicking at his self-pitched ball. (Stickball, Punchball, Kickball.)
Gotcha:	Common expression used in Tag, when a victim is caught by arms, legs, thighs, etc.
Grounder:	Ball hit and bouncing along the ground.
Hindu:	Verbal code for interference, do-over, etc., from the word hinderance, hinder.
Hockey Jock:	One who loves hockey more than the opposite sex or TV.
I dare you:	Psychological pressure exerted on obstinate players, in order to manipulate them into self-destructive feats.
Idiot's Tag:	Endless process of saying "Gotcha last" between two last candidates for "It."
In and Out the Window:	Game, accompanied by chant, of walking in and out a circle under joined hands.
Interference:	Technicality, such as wall, car, or object interrupting runner or ball in natural course of flight.

Jinksing:	Usually one player calls "No jinksies (or "jinksing") so as to bar any form of distraction, witchcraft, hexing, or psychological "tilt."
Knuckling down:	Resting on one's knuckles while shooting a marble.
Lagging:	Shooting from pitch line to lag line in order to determine which player shoots first (calling "first" is easier).
LMNOP:	Word stuck in the middle of the alphabet.
Me!:	Ingratiating self-nomination, along the lines of "first." When so driven, some people repeat the phrase, "Me! Me! Me!" (usually achieving their ends -- as long as they shut up).
Mine!:	Call for a fly ball in the field in order to avoid confusion about which player should catch. (Two players running head-on for the ball, yelling "Mine!" simultaneously, however, add impact to the game.)
Monkey's Uncle:	Anyone losing a game (an early attitude toward Darwin's theory).
No Taxes (no nothing):	Seal of wager made by self-confident gamester, meaning no second chance -- the outcome is final.
Not me!:	Act of not "Me-ing" or negating "Me!" (*see* Me!)
Nudge:	Bothersome gentle nag.
Nuggie:	Two forefingers protruding from half-clenched fist thrust into skull of friend or enemy.
Nurd:	A disliked kid—for no defined reason.
Oly-Oly-Oxen-Free:	All-clear signal in Hide and Seek.
Potato:	(Sometimes pronounced ber-ta-ter, pah-tay-tah, etc.) Vegetable, as well as invaluable counting tool in choosing sides.
Potsy:	American Hopscotch.
Saluggi:	Keep Away played with article of clothing.
Schlub:	Messy, sloppy kid, even among normally messy, sloppy kids.
Schimelecha(el):	Circle.
Sewer:	Idiom for manhole cover.
Shooter:	Marble or aggie shot from the hand.
Short Line:	Line from which ball is served, in Handball, sixteen feet from the wall.
Silly-Billy:	Irritating giggler who can't exercise self-control during serious street game.

Snooger:	Close-miss in Marbles.
Slapsies:	Closed hands slapped together with opponent's head between them. Form of Flinch for the connoisseur (or complete dope).
Spaldeen:	The Spalding Pinkey.
Step in it:	Descriptive phrase of placing foot in extraneous waste products scattered about street and sidewalk.
Taw:	Obsolete name for shooter or Marbles.
The best:	Any game desired on the spur of the moment; instant gratification.
Times up:	Call meaning "time to get on with it," after break or at end of time out.
Townies:	People from next (or another) town, used in rural areas to instill feeling in opposing team of being outsiders.
Zapper:	Stinging pain when slapped.
Zilch:	Great mathematical scorekeeping invention devised by street players to indicate undignified non-achievement represented by zero, i.e., the score was twelve-zilch (twelve-to-nothing).

Index

About the Author

Alan Milberg, a graduate of Boston University with a B.A. degree in Philosophy and Religion, is presently serving as Child Life Director (Department of Pediatrics) at a metropolitan hospital in New York City. A composer in his own right, he has written both librettos and scores for The Joffrey Ballet and has recently completed a ballet on prisons. Mr. Milberg has a studio on the Upper West Side of New York.